CW00543067

1 MONTH OF FREE READING

at

www.ForgottenBooks.com

By purchasing this book you are eligible for one month membership to ForgottenBooks.com, giving you unlimited access to our entire collection of over 1,000,000 titles via our web site and mobile apps.

To claim your free month visit:
www.forgottenbooks.com/free898167

ISBN 978-0-265-84527-1
PIBN 10898167

OUR JUDICIARY

MARCH 1, 1929

FOREWORD

Acquaintanceship and association, supplemented by intensive personal interest, have provided for me unusual opportunities extending over a substantial number of years to observe the workings of the Courts of Pennsylvania and to become more or less familiar with the personnel of the Judiciary.

My interest in the legal profession of **Pennsylvania** was instilled during childhood by admiration and high esteem for my late and honored father, J. A. Strassburger, former District Attorney of Montgomery County, and it has steadily been intensified with the passing of years by direct contact with many of the jurists who have so ably served on the Bench of the Commonwealth.

As the result of surveys, based on personal experience and observation, I am convinced the salaries of the judges should be substantially increased in order that the compensation be sufficient to provide not only the necessities of life, but also all other essentials as measured by the proper standards of their stations in life.

It is trite to say that without the Pennsylvania judicial system our political institutions could not be what they are, or possibly could not have endured until now.

It is not the individual judge the public thinks of, but the system of which he is a part. Hence, in addition to sound judicial decisions the character, the industry, the sincerity, the unquestioned integrity of the men who sit on the Bench have been and are essential qualifications for the judiciary; nothing is more vital for them to do than to uphold and enhance the dignity and the weight of the judiciary. I am glad to state the history of Pennsylvania's judiciary has been marked by a virtually unbroken and unmarred display of and adherence to the highest sense of justice and personal qualities, which, with correct judicial conduct, accompanied by a superlative degree of learning, diligence and unfailing sense of duty have won the unanimous testimony of approval of the public as well as members of all the county bar associations throughout more than one and a half centuries.

In recent years, it has been almost an impossibility, many judges find, of properly supporting their families and educating their children on present low salaries.

Only those judges who are so financially situated that they can supplement their salaries from their private incomes will be able to afford to stay on the Bench in years to come unless their compensation is placed on an adequate basis.

It is a fine testimonial to Pennsylvania to say that we have such able, talented jurists on the Bench of the State and that the Pennsylvania Judiciary is composed of splendid, patriotic men, but it is not fair to them, nor to the public, to make them sacrifice private practice that would produce much greater monetary returns than their present salaries.

The important work they do, the millions of dollars involved in the litigation which comes before them, the tremendous amount of physical and mental labor which they are called upon to perform, entitle them to at least a compensation which will, to some extent, relieve them of the worries and discomforts which must follow the present inadequate salaries.

The courts are one of the most important factors in our government and only the ablest, collectively speaking, have occupied positions on the Bench of Pennsylvania. These men, whose characters and abilities would earn them tens of thousands of dollars, and in some instances hundreds of thousands of dollars per year, are called upon to give their services for $7,000 to $12,000 a year, in the Common Pleas Courts and Orphans Courts in the various judicial districts of the State Courts based on population figures. The same is true of the judges of the Superior Court who now receive $16,000 per year, and the judges of the Supreme Court who now receive $17,500 per year.

The judges' salaries should not be, as has marked the past at all too infrequent intervals, slightly increased but substantially increased—their salaries should be raised at least 50 to 100 per cent.

It is my hope that the State Legislature will see its way clear to act promptly on this important legislation during its 1929 sessions at Harrisburg. And I also call upon lawyers, business men and citizens in all walks of life in all parts of the state to actively support the proposed legislation as every one should recognize the importance of keeping able and impartial judges on the Bench which is only possible in the years to come by paying them adequate salaries.

While I recognize the question of salary increases as a paramount question for immediate attention and action of the State Legislature, I can not forego this opportunity to say a word anent the congestion in the calendars of the Courts of Pennsylvania. This is also one of the major problems for future weal of the Commonwealth, which demands an early solution.

The flood of cases requiring trials before juries is mounting each year. An impartial survey reveals that the crowding of the court calendars of Pennsylvania is the direct outcome of the prohibition laws and the almost innumerable laws enacted in their wake and having sole bearing upon the liquor situation. It can not be attributed to any other special cause nor can it be blamed upon any particular tendency to litigation or criminality on the part of the people of Pennsylvania.

Findings of the Pennsylvania Crime Commission and other investigating groups conducted in the hope of relieving the congestion in the courts as well as obtaining a modern criminal code, indicate the growth of litigation in the courts of Pennsylvania may be expected to continue and all reports stress that a remedy must be sought and obtained without further delay.

It is generally realized by these investigators the burdens of the judges are increased immeasurably by the outworn laws that remain on the statute books. It is apparent that once having made a law, we are reluctant to admit its adoption was an error even should the law prove to be unworkable or otherwise undesirable and because of this attitude the statute books of Pennsylvania are cluttered up with "dead laws." I cite in particular the old blue laws. Few, if any of them, have ever been repealed, hence they lie buried in the dusty shelves of the law libraries. Students of jurisprudence find many other laws that were buried in the statute books without benefit of clergy, without the formal obsequies of "an act to repeal 'an act entitled,'" etc. These laws are inoperative because prosecuting attorneys recognized long ago they had outlived their usefulness, that they never could have been applied to any beneficial purpose or that they were absurd, ridiculous from the very beginning.

Too much of the judges' time, in my opinion, is also taken up by signing of orders most of them merely formal, that could be entrusted to a calendar clerk. Relieving the judges of minor administrative duties would be a forward step in improving present congested conditions.

Therefore, this historical series of "Montgomery County's Judiciary" will have served its purpose if it acts as a reminder to the public of the calibre of men, dead and living, who have so capably, efficiently, honestly and fearlessly presided on the Bench of Montgomery county since Frederick A. Muhlenberg was sworn in as the first judge of the county in 1784.

It was especially compiled to emphasize the worth of this group of men—which has its counterpart in all sections of this great and glorious commonwealth of Pennyslvania. It was published as deserved tribute to the service of these outstanding men in public office who have maintained respect for the judiciary at substantial sacrifices to themselves and their families.

In conclusion, I also express the hope it will focus attention on the urgency of introducing a bill for salary increases for all the judges of all the courts of Pennsylvania, as well as aiding to some small degree in encouraging an early simplification and clarification of the laws of the State, with resultant elimination of technicalities, reduction of formal court procedure to a minimum and the expediting of the wheels of justice.

RALPH BEAVER STRASSBURGER.

MONTGOMERY COUNTY'S JUDICIARY

❦ ❦ ❦

Historical Series Reprinted from the
Times Herald, Norristown, Pa.

FREDERICK A. MUHLENBERG

MONTGOMERY COUNTY'S judiciary, throughout the entire period of almost a century and a half that the county has been in existence, has always exemplified the best traditions of the bench. Virtually without exception, from the time of Frederick A. Muhlenberg down to the present, the judges who presided over the courts in Norristown gained the esteem of the community and the respect of the members of the bar for their high principles of honor and justice.

Moreover nearly all of these judges fulfilled the exalted duties of their office at the cost of personal financial sacrifice, for, since the time when it was required that the president judge must be a lawyer, there was not one of the judges who could not have derived a larger income from the practice of the law than he received as salary for his judicial services.

When Montgomery county's first Court of Common Pleas was held, December 28, 1784, judicial procedure varied greatly from that now in effect. It was not necessary then that judges should be learned in the law. Lawyers were few in Pennsylvania, and strong popular prejudice existed against the profession. The possession of high standards of common honesty and common sense were deemed much more requisite for a judge than knowledge of the intricacies of the law.

According to the regulations of that time all justices of the peace holding office in Montgomery county were constituted judges of the court when Montgomery county came into existence by action of the Pennsylvania Assembly, September 10, 1784. There were at that time seven justices of the peace in the county, each of whom had jurisdiction over several townships. These justices and their districts were:

Frederick A. Muhlenberg, of Trappe, for Providence, Limerick and Perkiomen and Skippack Townships. Providence consisted of the present Upper and Lower Providence. The two townships now known as Perkiomen and Skippack were then one township with the double name.

Michael Croll, of Upper Salford Township, for that township and also Marlborough and Upper Hanover.

John Richards, of Upper Hanover Township, for that township, as well as Frederick and Douglass.

Peter Evans, of Montgomery Township, for that township and also Gwynedd and Hatfield.

James Morris, of Whitpain Township, for that township, Norriton and Worcester.

William Dean, of Moreland, for Moreland, Upper Dublin and Horsham.

Henry Scheetz, of Whitemarsh Township, for Whitemarsh, Springfield and Plymouth.

The office was vacant in the district comprising Lower Salford, Franconia and Towamencin, while Abington and Cheltenham were part of a district which included townships in Philadelphia county, the justice living in Bristol township, Philadelphia, and Upper and Lower Merion likewise were in a district whose justice lived in Blockley Township, Philadelphia.

Under the Act of Assembly creating the new county, these justices therefore constituted the court of the county. Any three of them could hold the Court of Quarter Sessions, Common Pleas and General Jail Delivery, and Orphans' Court. They had jurisdiction over all manner of cases excepting only felonies for which the punishment was death. Such felonies at that time included not only murder, but also counterfeiting, burglary and other crimes. Cases of this character were to be tried by judges of the Supreme Court of the state on circuit. The Supreme Court judges were men learned in the law.

Just where the first session of the Court of Common Pleas of Montgomery County was held, has been a matter of dispute among historians. The minutes as pre-

served fix the date as December 28, 1784. According to
the record the court was held "at the house of John
Shannon." Prior to this time John Shannon conducted
the Barley Sheaf tavern, on the Manatawny or Germantown road, in Norriton Township, northwest of Stony
Creek. In March, 1785, he was assessed as owner of a
tavern on Egypt road, now Main street, Norristown,
east of Stony Creek.

According to a tradition in the Shannon family, the
first court was held in the barn at the Barley Sheaf
tavern. That version is accepted by most histories of the
county. Yet it was clear from the time the county was
constituted that the county-seat was to be near the con-
fluence of Stony Creek with the Schuylkill, and since
John Shannon had a tavern in that locality there seems
reason for doubting that the court would meet on Germantown road.

The record of licenses issued to John Shannon gives
no help, as his residence is merely noted as Norriton
Township, and both the tavern sites mentioned were in
Norriton Township.

According to the minutes the justices present at the
session of court were F. A. Muhlenberg, James Morris,
John Richards, Henry Scheetz and William Dean.

Upon the opening of court, at 12 o'clock noon, the
commissions of the justices were read and also that of
Thomas Craig as clerk of the court.

Members of the grand jury were then sworn, and
Justice Muhlenberg charged them. The constables of the
several townships made their returns. Only two cases
were adjudicated, these being disputes between township
poor boards over the care of paupers whose residence
was a matter of uncertainty.

While this session on December 28, 1784, was the
first of the Court of Common Pleas, it was not the first
transaction of court business in the new county. A session of the Orphans' Court was held at Trappe on December 1 of that year, with Justices Muhlenberg, Richards,
Morris and Scheetz present.

It is not clear from documentary evidence just how Frederick A. Muhlenberg became president judge. He was recognized as such, however, from the establishment of the court until September, 1785. Under the Pennsylvania constitution of that time the president judge was to be appointed by the Supreme Executive Council of the state. The Council never appointed Muhlenberg. Apparently he served by the common consent of the other justices.

The act establishing the county designated commissioners to erect county buildings. The contract for the court house and prison was not awarded until August, 1785, and the trustees of the University of Pennsylvania, did not give the deed for the site of the court house and prison until December following.

Thus so long as Frederick A. Muhlenberg presided over the courts these courts had no home of their own. According to the minutes the sessions of March and June, 1785, were again held at "the house of John Shannon," while in September, 1785, the court met "in Norris Town," though the building is not mentioned.

When Frederick A. Muhlenberg became the first president judge of Montgomery county, he was one of Pennsylvania's best known citizens. Several years' participation in the turbulent politics of the State Assembly had caused him to repent, at least for the time being, that he had taken up public activities, and he sought to retire to the quietude of his home at Trappe, serving his neighbors in the capacity of justice of the peace. He had held that office but a short time when the new county was created and events shaped themselves so as to bring about Muhlenberg's return to official service.

Motives of patriotism induced Frederick A. Muhlenberg to forsake the ministry at the time of the Revolution and take up a career in political life, just as his brother Peter also discarded the robe of the clergyman for the uniform of the military commander.

At Trappe, where his father, Rev. Henry Melchior Muhlenberg lived and directed the endeavors of the Lutheran congregations from New York to Georgia,

Frederick A. Muhlenberg was born on January 1, 1750. Conrad Weiser, father of Mrs. Muhlenberg, was a guest in the home at Trappe at the time. In his honor, as well as in tribute to two clerical friends of the father abroad, the son, at his baptism in Augustus Church two weeks after his birth, was named Conrad Frederick Augustus Muhlenberg. In later life he wrote his name Frederick A. Muhlenberg.

The father destined his three sons for the ministry, and in 1763, he sent them to Halle, in Germany, to be educated. Peter, the eldest, was then 15; Frederick was 13, and Gotthilf Heinrich was only 10. Only the two younger sons followed out the father's plans. Peter, preferring business to theology, had a series of unpleasant experiences in Germany and then returned home, where the father's desire to make him a clergyman finally prevailed. Frederick and his youngest brother Henry returned to America in 1770, and both were ordained to the Lutheran ministry, notwithstanding their youth. Henry, the youngest son, was the only one who continued in the ministry throughout his life, though he was also famous as a botanist.

Frederick A. Muhlenberg's first pastoral assignment was as assistant to his brother-in-law, Rev. Christian Emanuel Schulze, in the Tulpehocken region. In 1773 he became pastor of Christ Church, New York. As the Revolution opened his support of the American cause was so outspoken that when the British gained possession of the city he and his family found it advisable to leave.

In 1771 Muhlenberg had married Catherine, daughter of David Schaefer, of Philadelphia, a sugar refiner who was an elder of Zion's Lutheran Church in that city. After a stay in Philadelphia in the summer of 1776, Muhlenberg and his family repaired to Trappe. On August 23 he preached to Captain Richards' company, from New Hanover, then leaving to join the American army. Shortly after that he and his family made their home at New Hanover, Muhlenberg assisting his father in ministering to the Lutheran congregations there and at Oley, New Goshenhoppen and Reading.

Thus Muhlenberg was engaged when the British army invaded Pennsylvania, in 1777. Fugitives from Philadelphia often crowded his home. In September the American army, in which his brother Peter commanded a brigade, was encamped in the neighborhood, first at Pottsgrove and later along the Perkiomen where Schwenksville now is. In a letter written from New Hanover on September 30, 1777, Muhlenberg informed his brother-in-law, Pastor Schulze, in Tulpehocken, that "Our general (Peter Muhlenberg) is well. Yesterday Burkhard, Schaefer and I slept with him in camp. The army stands ten miles distant from here and three miles from the Trappe."

No doubt the course of his brother Peter in forsaking the pulpit for the army had deep influence upon Frederick A. Muhlenberg. Early in 1779 he resolved to relinquish the ministry and give himself to public service. Three vacancies existed in Pennsylvania's delegation in the Continental Congress. On March 2, 1779, the Pennsylvania Assembly filled these vacancies, naming Frederick A. Muhlenberg for one of them. The congressional term expired in the fall, and in November Muhlenberg was one of five members elected to Congress in Pennsylvania.

In Congress Muhlenberg was made chairman of the medical committee, which exercised supervision over the military hospitals.

At the next election, in October, 1780, Muhlenberg was elected to the State Assembly, and when the Assembly convened he was made speaker, retaining that office for the two succeeding sessions. A further honor was accorded him in 1783 when he was made president of the board of censors, a peculiar institution of that time which passed on the laws and finances of the state.

Apparently there were moments during his legislative duties in Philadelphia when Muhlenberg regretted having left the ministry. In a letter written in 1780 were these words: "I have no horse, nor can I afford to keep one. Believe me, I am not so well off now as when I left the Swamp, and if I had not been induced by the urgent appeals of the Germans to accept membership in the Assembly, a resolution in which the large majority of votes I received further confirmed me, I might have been tempted to take again to the apostolate. But I am here not my own master, and must be satisfied to serve where my fellow citizens want me."

In 1783 the German Lutheran congregation in Ebenezer, Georgia, made overtures to have Muhlenberg become its pastor, but they proved fruitless.

Muhlenberg joined with a man named Wegman in establishing a store on Second street, near Arch, Philadelphia. But he longed to return to Trappe. He bought a stone house and 50 acres at Trappe of Herman Reid in 1781. Upon the expiration of his term in the Assembly, in 1784, he declined re-election, writing: "Henceforward I shall have nothing to do with public office. I am justice of the peace and can be serviceable to my neighbors. My store is doing well and is in good running order."

His retirement did not endure long. In the establishment of the new county of Montgomery he could not be overlooked. Even before the court convened and he became president judge, the Supreme Executive Council appointed him register of wills and recorder of deeds of the new county. He entered upon those duties on October 19, when he recorded a deed and two mortgages and also granted letters of administration in the estate of a resident of New Hanover Township. He held these offices until 1789. The office of justice of the peace he resigned in 1788.

Many higher honors still awaited him. When a convention was called, in 1787, to determine Pennsylvania's attitude with regard to the proposed constitution for the United States, Muhlenberg was elected a delegate, and when the convention assembled in Philadelphia, he was made its presiding officer. The convention, after three weeks' session, approved the constitution, and this action was of far-reaching influence at a critical moment in national affairs, for chaos had developed under the old system of confederation.

At the first election of members of the National House of Representatives under the constitution both Frederick A. Muhlenberg and his brother, General Peter Muhlenberg, were chosen among the eight members from Pennsylvania. Now with every circumstance of honor and triumph Muhlenberg returned to New York, whence he had been compelled to flee 13 years earlier because of his patriotism.

Upon the organization of the First Congress Muhlenberg's executive ability was recognized by his election as speaker. He continued as a member of the Second, Third and Fourth Congresses, and was speaker of the Third. Both of the Muhlenbergs were staunch supporters of Thomas Jefferson and the anti-Federalist movement, and their efforts were largely responsible in making Jefferson's party dominant in Pennsylvania.

The last office that Muhlenberg held was that of collector general of the land office of Pennsylvania, he receiving this appointment from Governor McKean in 1800. The duties of the office required him to live in Lancaster, then the seat of the state's government. In that city his brother Henry was pastor of the Lutheran congregation. However, death cut short Frederick A. Muhlenberg's career on June 4, 1801. He was buried in Lancaster.

From 1779 until 1786, Muhlenberg was one of the trustees of the University of Pennsylvania; and he was president of the German Society of Pennsylvania from 1789 until 1797.

The most famous of Frederick A. Muhlenberg's descendants was his grandson, Rev. Dr. William A. Muhlenberg, a distinguished divine of the Episcopal faith who served churches in Lancaster, Philadelphia and New York and who is remembered chiefly as a writer of hymns, two of the best known being "I Would Not Live Alway" and "Saviour, Who Thy Flock Art Feeding"

JAMES MORRIS

HIGH standards which have been maintained ever since were set for the Montgomery county judiciary when a man of the outstanding distinction of Frederick A. Muhlenberg served as the first president judge, following the organization of the county, in 1784. He held the office not quite one year. But his successor was also a man possessed of notable qualifications, though he did not receive the national recognition accorded to Muhlenberg, and, strange to say, is given slight mention in the books on Montgomery county history.

According to the law of that time, the justices of the peace of a county constituted the county's board of judges, and the Supreme Executive Council of the state appointed the president judge. No commission as president judge was ever issued to Muhlenberg. He seemed to have served by the unanimous consent of the justices. However, on July 23, 1785, the Supreme Executive Council issued a commission to James Morris, of Dawesfield, in Whitpain Township, as "president of the court of Common Pleas and of the Court of General Quarter Sessions of the Peace" of Montgomery county. He held the office for four years.

Muhlenberg, though no longer president judge, continued to serve as one of the justices until his election to Congress, in 1788. To the seven justices of the peace who were in office when the first court met, in 1784, several were added during the time that James Morris was presiding judge. The first justices, each of whom had jurisdiction over several townships, were: Michael Croll, Upper Salford; William Dean, Moreland; Frederick A. Muhlenberg Providence; John Richards, New Hanover; Henry Scheetz, Whitemarsh; James Morris, Whitpain, and Peter Evans, of Montgomery.

In 1786 Christian Weber, of Towamencin, was elected for the district comprising Towamencin, Lower

Salford and Franconia. The same year Abington and Cheltenham, previously linked to Bristol Township, Philadelphia county, were constituted a district, Jonathan Shoemaker being elected justice; while Upper and Lower Merion, which had made a district with Blockley Township, Philadelphia, also formed a new district, the justice elected being John Jones.

Another new district was laid out in the western corner of the county, comprising what later became the borough of Pottstown and Upper and Lower Pottsgrove Townships. Here John Hockley was made justice. In addition John Pugh and Henry Pawling were commissioned as additional justices of the peace for "Norris Town." When Muhlenberg resigned as justice, in 1788, Anthony Crothers was appointed his successor.

These men therefore constituted the board of judges up to 1790, and any three of them were competent to hold court. None of them was trained in the law.

In this period Montgomery county had its first trial of a case involving a capital offense. Such cases, according to the regulations of that time, had to be tried by judges of the Supreme Court of the state.

The accused men were Philip Hoofnagle and John Brown, who were charged with burglary, an offense then punishable with death. Justices Atlee and Bryan, of the Supreme Court, came to Norristown to hold Court on October 11, 1786. Among the members of the grand jury summoned for the term were two of the Montgomery county board of judges, Frederick A. Muhlenberg, the first president judge, and his successor, James Morris.

Hoofnagle was convicted of burglary, but escaped the death penalty, being sentenced to five years' imprisonment. The trial of Brown was postponed until the following March. When Brown was brought before the court for trial, Chief Justice McKean and Justice Bryan were on the bench. Brown was convicted and sentenced to be hanged. It is said his own refusal to avail himself of a new law compelled the judges to pronounce sentence of death. The case aroused much excitement in

Norristown, chiefly because of a controversy over the selection of a place for erecting the gallows. Some citizens resented the desire to make the hanging a public spectacle. An appeal to the Supreme Executive Council was in vain, and Brown shortly forfeited his life.

When he became president judge of Montgomery county James Morris was but 32 years old. He had already served in the Pennsylvania Assembly for two terms, in 1782 and 1783. During the American Revolution his activities in behalf of the American cause were such as to arouse the censure of Gwynedd Monthly Meeting of Friends, he being a birthright member of the Society of Friends.

He was commissioned third lieutenant in the Pennsylvania Regiment of Artillery on April 1, 1777. While president judge of Montgomery county he was captain of the Montgomery County Troop of Light Horse, and he commanded that troop in a parade in Philadelphia on July 4, 1788. He was appointed brigadier general of the Montgomery county militia in 1793, and the following year he participated in the expedition to suppress the "Whisky Insurrection" in Western Pennsylvania.

While he was president judge he was elected, in 1787, as a delegate to the Pennsylvania convention to ratify the new federal constitution. Over this convention Frederick A. Muhlenberg presided.

Judge Morris also was a member of the convention that met in 1789 and 1790 to formulate a new constitution for Pennsylvania.

In 1791 Governor Mifflin appointed him register of wills and recorder of deeds of Montgomery county, and in 1792 he was a Presidential elector.

Perhaps of all the honors that came to James Morris none was esteemed more highly, either by him or his descendants, than the fact that he was Washington's host for two weeks during the desperate times of the Pennsylvania campaign in the Revolution. It was after the battle of Germantown, when the army, having retreated to the banks of the Perkiomen, moved first into Towamencin, then into Worcester and on October 19, 1777, into Whitpain and Upper Dublin Townships. Washington then made his headquarters at Dawesfield, the home of James Morris, in the eastern part of Whitpain Township, remaining there until November 2, when the army advanced to Whitemarsh Township.

Dawesfield has ever since been the home of descendants of James Morris. It is situated west of the borough of Ambler, on Lewis lane, between Skippack pike and Morris road. The last named road testifies to the long-time prominence of the Morris family in that region. Mr. and Mrs. George J. Cooke now occupy the noted old house, Mrs. Cooke being of the eighth generation of the family that has dwelt at Dawesfield.

The house, though enlarged since the days of the Revolution, contains many treasures of that time, among them the bedstead and other furniture which Washington used, the chair in which General Lafayette sat while here recovering from his wound received at Brandywine and a lock of Washington's hair.

The chief occurrence during the time the house was the headquarters of General Washington was the court martial of General Anthony Wayne for his management of his forces when the British overwhelmed him at Paoli, the preceding month. After several days' session the court completely vindicated Wayne.

Anthony Morris, grandfather of James Morris, bought a large tract of land including what was later the Dawesfield property, in 1713. In 1726 he sold 400 acres to Abraham Dawes, and five years later Abraham Dawes, Jr., became the owner. He built the house in 1736. His daughter Elizabeth married James Morris in 1772.

At the time of his marriage, James Morris was living on a farm adjoining Dawesfield at what is now the southwest corner of Butler pike and Morris road. His father, Joseph Morris, had bought a mill and 94 acres of land here in 1771 and placed his son James in charge.

A pleasing tradition tells how James Morris and Elizabeth Dawes became interested in each other. She was riding down Morris road on horseback, when James Morris, also on horseback, came the other way. When the two horses met the young woman's animal turned about and seemed determined to accompany the other horse. Miss Dawes explained to the young man that this was a chronic bad habit of her horse. Whenever he met another horse going the opposite way he would turn about and insist on accompanying the other horse. She asked Morris to escort her home to avoid further obstreptrousness on the part of her horse. Of course he was happy to comply. Thus began the acquaintance that led to their marriage.

For five years the couple lived in Morris' house. Then they made their home at Dawesfield. Morris built another mill on the Dawesfield estate. It is said he used timber for the purpose that had been felled in the nearby woods when the army was in camp there. Both of Morris' mills stood until about 40 years ago.

A son John, born in 1775, accompanied his father in the military expedition for the suppression of the "Whisky Insurrection" in 1794. Shortly after his return he was drenched with water in fighting a fire at a nearby church. This, together with the hardships incurred on the military expedition, affected his health, so that his death ensued on July 1, 1796.

James Morris himself died the preceding year, July 10, 1795, when but 42 years old. He was buried at Plymouth Meeting.

Besides the son who died in 1796, James Morris had a daughter. She became the wife of Dr. Thomas C. James. Their daughter, Phoebe M., married Saunders Lewis, and she and her husband lived at Dawesfield for many years, Mrs. Lewis dying there in 1902. Elizabeth Morris Lewis, daughter of Mr. and Mrs. Saunders Lewis, married Colonel George G. Meade, son of General Meade, of Civil War fame. The daughter of Colonel and Mrs. Meade is the present Mrs. George J. Cooke, of Dawesfield.

JAMES BIDDLE

FOR seven years following the establishment of Montgomery county, in 1784, the justices of the peace in the county constituted the judges of the county's courts, the services of a judge learned in the law being required only in criminal cases in which the death penalty could be invoked. Such cases were tried by judges of the Supreme Court on circuit.

This was the arrangement under the constitution which Pennsylvania adopted in 1776, immediately after the Declaration of Independence brought the new American nation into existence. Hastily planned as it **was and** yielding in many details to the passions and prejudices of wartime conditions, this first constitution of Pennsylvania as a state never worked satisfactorily, and after the nation had found it expedient to discard the original system of confederation and devise a new constitution, the state of Pennsylvania also set about formulating a new set of basic principles for its government. The outcome was the constitution of 1790.

Under this constitution the jurisdiction of justices of the peace was restricted to the districts for which they were commissioned, and they no longer had authority to hold court for the county. Instead, the state was divided into judicial districts, each consisting of three to six counties. Each district was to have a president judge who was to be learned in the law. The governor was to appoint the president judges. In addition there were to be associate judges for each county. They were not required to be lawyers. The number of such associate judges was to be "not less than three nor more than four" in each county.

According to this new arrangement Montgomery county was included in the First Judicial District, along with the counties of Philadelphia, Bucks and Delaware.

For president judge in this district Governor Thomas
Mifflin appointed James Biddle.

James Biddle was one of a noted Pennsylvania
family, several of whose members rendered distinguished
public service in the Revolutionary period and whose descendants have since held foremost rank socially in
Philadelphia. His brother Edward was a member of the
Continental Congress. Another brother, Nicholas, was
an officer in the navy. Charles, a third brother, was vice-
president of Pennsylvania when Benjamin Franklin was
president, before the adoption of the constitution of 1790.
Charles Biddle was the father of Nicholas Biddle, the
famous Philadelphia banker of the early nineteenth century who as president of the United States Bank led the
fight against President Andrew Jackson's endeavors to
strangle this and all other banking institutions in the
land.

James Biddle was the son of William and Mary
Scull Biddle. His mother was a daughter of Nicholas
Scull, famous Surveyor General of Provincial Pennsylvania who was a resident of Whitemarsh Township. At
the time of his appointment as president judge he was
60 years old.

He had read law with John Ross, the foremost
Philadelphia lawyer of his day. He then located in Reading and practiced law in Berks, Lancaster and Northampton counties until 1760. Then he moved to Philadelphia to become deputy prothonotary, and later he was
made deputy judge of the admiralty in the royal government. When this government was swept out of existence
by the Revolution, Biddle returned to Reading and resumed the practice of law there.

After the Revolution he was suggested for the Supreme Court of the state. The judges of that court were
elected for seven-year terms by the Supreme Executive
Council. On the expiration of the term of Judge Bryan,
some of Biddle's friends wanted to make him Bryan's
successor. This, it was thought, could easily be accomplished because his brother Charles was then vice-president of the state and influential in political matters. Re-

garding this project Charles Biddle wrote in his auto-biography:

"Although he was as dear to me as it was possible for one brother to be to another, for he had been more than a father to me, I could not think of using any interest I had against Mr. Bryan."

However, in 1788, James Biddle received the appointment of prothonotary in Philadelphia, a lucrative office.

Judge Bryan died in 1791, and then Charles Biddle felt his brother could with entire propriety be advanced to the Supreme Court. But Governor Mifflin gave the office to Edward Shippen, then president judge of the Philadelphia courts. A sharp controversy ensued over the matter between the governor and Charles Biddle. As a compromise Governor Mifflin proposed to name James Biddle as Judge Shippen's successor, though under the new constitution then effective he would be president judge not only of Philadelphia but also of the three additional counties of the judicial district.

The suggestion did not please Charles Biddle. "He must have known," he wrote, alluding to the governor, "the office was worth very little and my brother should not with my consent accept it."

But when the governor interviewed James Biddle he concluded to take the judgship thus offered.

"I insisted, however," Charles Biddle noted, "upon my brother receiving the emoluments of the prothonotary's office until a further provision was made for the office he was to have, which was soon after done."

Thus it is evident that the inadequate pay of judges is by no means an issue of recent development.

As James Biddle became president judge the office of prothonotary which he vacated was given to his brother Charles, he having lost the vice-presidency of the state when the new constitution went into effect, substituting a governor for the president and vice-president elected by the Supreme Executive Council.

James Biddle remained on the bench of his four-county district until his death, in 1797.

As to his services in a judicial capacity little re-
mains on record. His brother's autobiography notes that
at the time of the yellow fever epidemic of 1793 in Philadelphia, Judge Biddle, after first making his will, went
into the city at the time designated for the September
session of court. He formally opened court but quickly
adjourned it. Only five lawyers were present in court.
Two of these remained in the city for the purpose of
writing wills. Both of them were stricken with the
fever and died.

Judge Biddle made periodical visits to the three
counties of his district outside Philadelphia to hold court,
the sessions for Delaware county being held in Chester,
those for Bucks county in Newtown, while Norristown,
then as now, was the countyseat of Montgomery county.

On June 13, 1797, Judge Biddle came to Norristown
to hold court. He went to his home in Philadelphia at
night feeling fatigued. In the night he became sick, and
two days later he was dead. He was buried in the grounds
of Christ Church, Philadelphia. Since 1776 he had been
a vestryman of Christ Church.

JOHN D. COXE AND WILLIAM TILGHMAN

JOHN D. COXE, who became president judge of the district of which Montgomery county was a part, in 1797, upon the death of Judge James Biddle, was, like his predecessor, a member of a family that has long been conspicuous in the civic and social annals of Philadelphia and Pennsylvania.

Surprisingly little, however, is known about John D. Coxe. No anecdotes have come down through the years tending to depict his characteristics. No noted trials are associated with his name.

One curious fact concerning Judge Coxe is that his name was simply John Coxe, but he inserted the "D" to give the name an element of distinction, though the letter did not represent any name.

He was born in 1752, studied at the College of Philadelphia and entered the bar. He served from 1797 until 1805 as president judge of the judicial district embracing Montgomery, Bucks, Delaware and Philadelphia counties. From 1800 until 1805 he was also president judge of the Second Judicial District, comprising Chester, Lancaster, York and Dauphin counties. Thus his duties required him to travel over a large part of the state.

After retiring from the bench Judge Coxe was for a time a trustee of the University of Pennsylvania. He lived retired for many years, dying in 1824.

Horace Binney, famous Philadelphia lawyer, wrote thus of Judge Coxe: "He was a sound lawyer and a very honest man, a little too much disturbed by his doubts and his talent for making distinctions, but on the whole very safe, very patient and very well tempered. I could tell when a doubt had seized him by the manner in which he pulled his eyebrows, as if he could disentangle the web by straightening the hairs."

Tench Coxe, long a leader in politics and business affairs, was a younger brother of Judge Coxe. Tench Coxe was a member of the Continental Congress, assistant secretary of the treasury, leader of the Republican Party in his day and he gave valuable services toward the development of American manufactures in the early days of the republic.

A daughter of Judge Coxe married John G. Watmough, who served with distinction in the War of 1812, and who lived for a time in Hope Lodge, the famous colonial mansion on Bethlehem pike, Whitemarsh.

A man who, like Judge Biddle and Judge Coxe, was one of an outstanding family and who himself was destined to become a shining light of the American bench, became president judge upon the death of Judge Coxe. This was William Tilghman. He occupied the office less than a year.

Judge Tilghman was in his 50th year when he was appointed president judge of the First Judicial District. He had already served the public in numerous capacities. The highest honor to which he attained was that of chief judge of the United States Circuit Court for Pennsylvania, Delaware and New Jersey. However, this honor was fraught with embarrassment for Tilghman, and finally, because of political wrangles, the office was wrested from him.

Toward the end of the eighteenth century and the beginning of the nineteenth, the powers of the courts and the functions of the judges were made a political issue. The followers of Thomas Jefferson, sometimes called Democrats, sometimes Republicans and occasionally Democrat-Republicans, resisted what they believed was a tendency toward autocracy on the part of the judiciary. Numerous attempts were made to strip the courts of their powers. One outcome of these controversies was the passage of a law in Congress in February, 1801, reducing the number of Supreme Court judges to five, but creating circuit courts. This was a victory for the Federalists, who believed in strengthening the judiciary.

In the last hours of his term President John Adams rushed to the Senate the appointment of a number of new circuit court judges, one of whom was William Tilghman. Because of their late appointment these judges were popularly known as the "midnight judges."

Tilghman assumed the bench. But in April, 1802, Jefferson's followers being in power in Congress, they repealed the act establishing the circuit courts, and thus Judge Tilghman was legislated out of office.

Tilghman was a native of Maryland who came to Philadelphia in 1760 and studied law under Benjamin Chew, later chief justice of the province. He practiced law for ten years in Maryland, was a member of the Maryland Assembly and then of the Senate, and in 1793 he returned to Philadelphia to practice law.

His brief service as president judge of the First Judicial District, in 1805 and 1806, was terminated by his appointment as chief justice of the Supreme Court of Pennsylvania, to succeed Edward Shippen. Here he won honor and renown. It fell to him to establish many principles of law, especially in applying the common law of England here in the United States. Brilliancy and dash were not his characteristics, but for patient, thorough and accurate analysis he has had few superiors on the bench. Among lawyers he is remembered chiefly for his twenty volumes of Reports, embodying 2000 judgments which he pronounced.

His services to the bench and bar were recognized when Harvard College bestowed upon him the degree of doctor of laws. He was president of the American Philosophical Society and the first president of the Philadelphia Athenaeum.

Justice Tilghman warmly espoused the effort to foster American industries when that cause became prominent at the time of the War of 1812. He was president of the Society for the Encouragement of American Manufactures. It is said that during the last ten years of his life he refused to wear any kind of imported clothing. And that meant much more then than now, for America was then dependent to a marked degree upon Europe for nearly all manner of wearing apparel.

BIRD WILSON

MONTGOMERY COUNTY remained in the same judicial district with Philadelphia county from the time the system of judicial districts under the constitution of 1790 became effective until 1806. Then Philadelphia was made an independent district, while Chester county was added to the three counties formerly linked with Philadelphia—Delaware, Bucks and Montgomery. The new district was numbered the Seventh.

Judge William Tilghman, who had been president judge for less than a year, was elevated to the office of chief justice of the Pennsylvania Supreme Court about this time. Bird Wilson was then appointed president judge of the new Seventh Judicial District.

Judge Wilson lent distinction to the judiciary. That he possessed marked individuality is evident from the many stories about him which have survived to the present time. He is chiefly remembered for the fact that he resigned the office of judge to become a minister of the gospel. Thus he reversed the course of Montgomery county's first president judge, for Frederick A. Muhlenberg was first a minister but forsook that calling for public life.

The sixth judge to preside over the courts in Montgomery county, Judge Wilson, nevertheless was the first to make his home in Norristown.

It is said he was the youngest judge learned in the law who was appointed to the bench up to that time in Pennsylvania, he being then in his 30th year. Sometimes there were intimations that he was not as learned in the law as he might have been. He probably never tried a case before a jury. Some accounts of his career declare that only once was his decision reversed in a higher court. However, among 22 appeals of his cases which are reported there were 11 reversals by the Supreme Court.

Nevertheless the high standard of Judge Wilson's life and his conscientious devotion to duty never have been questioned.

Splendid traits must have come to him by heredity, for he was the son of that James Wilson who was a signer of the Declaration of Independence, a member of the Continental Congress, a leader in the convention that framed the federal constitution, and the first justice of the United States Supreme Court appointed from Pennsylvania.

Bird Wilson was born in Carlisle, Pa., in 1777, studied at the University of Pennsylvania and was admitted to the Philadelphia bar in 1797. Instead of practicing law he took a position in the office of the commissioner of the bankruptcy law.

On assuming the duties of president judge, in 1806, he made his home in Norristown in a house where the Catholic Protectory now stands, the property extending from Main street to Sandy street, east of Walnut street. There Rev. Dr. J. G. Ralston established Oakland Female Institute in 1845 and conducted the school for more than 30 years.

Judge Wilson was noted for his methodical habits. He would walk five miles every day, sometimes over the roads of the vicinity, sometimes through his own grounds, and occasionally if the weather was unpropitious for outdoor activity he did his walking indoors.

As evidence of his kind-heartedness, it used to be said that he never permitted kittens that appeared on his place to be drowned. But the tradition continues that he was not averse to getting rid of the superabundant kittens by giving a hired man a bag full of them with instructions to lose them somewhere in the town.

The story of Judge Wilson's resignation from the bench, as usually told, is to the effect that he could not bring himself to impose the death sentence on a man convicted of murder, and rather than do so he resigned and entered the ministry. Examination of the records of the trial in question call for some modification of the generally accepted tradition.

John H. Craige, a blacksmith, shot and killed Edward Hunter, a justice of the peace in Delaware county. Motive was found in the fact that the "squire" had written the will of Craige's father-in-law and the will disinherited Craige. The crime occurred on July 19, 1817. The case never was tried before Judge Wilson. It came to trial in April, 1818, with Judge John Ross on the bench. Judge Ross had been made president judge of the district in February, 1818, Judge Wilson having resigned on January 1 of that year. The accused man was convicted, and Judge Ross pronounced the death sentence. Craige was hanged on June 6, 1818.

So far as can be ascertained Judge Wilson had taken the first steps toward entering the ministry of the Episcopal church some months before the murder occurred. It is probably true that he felt some compunctions about trying a murder case under these circumstances, and the approach of the trial may have hastened his resignation. However, he did try several murder cases during the time he was on the bench. He had hardly taken his seat when he pronounced sentence of death upon a woman who had killed her child.

At any rate Judge Wilson pursued theological studies under Bishop White, and his ordination followed. Here in Norristown he had helped to found St. John's Episcopal Church, in 1813, and became one of its wardens. Upon the death of Rev. Thomas P. May, rector of St. John's, Judge Wilson, in 1820, was made rector. The parish then comprised St. Thomas' Church, Whitemarsh, in addition to St. John's.

Though assiduous in pastoral duties, Judge Wilson lacked oratorical graces and his voice was weak. Consequently, after about two years' service in parish work, he found more congenial occupation as a professor of systematic divinity in the Episcopal General Theological Seminary, in New York. That position he held until 1850, when he was made emeritus professor.

In 1826 he was a candidate for assistant bishop in the Diocese of Pennsylvania, that office having been created to aid the aging Bishop White. Dr. Wilson received 26 votes in the convention to 27 for Rev. William Meade. It transpired later that Dr. Wilson had himself cast a blank vote, and this was the only blank vote. A controversy developed over the election, and it was declared null. When another election took place Dr. Wilson declined to be a candidate.

From 1829 until 1841 Dr. Wilson was secretary of the House of Bishops. He wrote voluminously on theological topics. His chief legal work is an "Abridgement of the Laws," in seven volumes.

Dr. Wilson never married. He taxed his resources for many years by providing for three brothers and two sisters.

His death occurred in 1859, and he was buried in the grounds of Christ Church, Philadelphia.

JOHN ROSS

WHILE Judge John Ross presided over the courts of Montgomery county, from 1818 until 1830, he proved himself a jurist of high attainments, and a man of striking personality. From him, moreover, has come a notable lineage, including a second Judge Ross who also graced the bench of Montgomery county.

The Rosses were a Bucks county family of Scotch-Irish ancestry, the first American progenitor having been a Thomas Ross, who settled in Upper Makefield Township in 1728 and who was a minister of the Society of Friends.

As a young man John Ross was a school teacher at Durham Furnace, along the Delaware in Bucks county. It is said Richard Backhouse, owner of Durham Furnace, recognizing the native talents of the young teacher, persuaded him to study law, offering to pay his expenses until he was able to support himself.

John Ross had a cousin, Thomas Ross, who was a successful lawyer in West Chester, and with him the Bucks county lad became a student. He began the practice of law in Easton, was soon made prothonotary of Northampton county, and was then elected to the State House of Representatives. Next he was chosen as member of Congress for the district comprising Northampton, Bucks, Lehigh, Wayne and Pike counties.

It was while he was a representative in Congress that Judge Bird Wilson resigned from the office of president judge of the judicial district comprising Montgomery, Chester, Delaware and Bucks counties, he having decided to enter the ministry of the Episcopal Church. Governor Findlay filled the vacancy early in 1818 by appointing John Ross.

Judge Ross' wife was a member of the Jenkins family for whom Jenkintown was named. At Jenkintown

they made their home soon after Judge Ross took his
seat upon the bench. Judge Ross used to drive to the
countyseats of the four counties in his district to hold
court, making the trip behind a pair of dappled horses
which were his favorites.

The four-county judicial district was divided in
1821 into two districts, and Judge Ross retained the new
district consisting of Bucks and Montgomery counties.
He now made his home in Doylestown, which place had
succeeded Newtown as the countyseat of Bucks county a
few years before. There was an old tavern near the new
court house. This property Judge Ross bought. He
converted the tavern into a commodious dwelling, and
there he and two following generations of the Ross
family lived until 1896, when the house was removed.

Judge Ross continued to preside over the courts of
Bucks and Montgomery counties until 1830, when Gov-
ernor Wolf appointed him to the Supreme Court of the
State.

Of the many anecdotes told about Judge Ross one
will suffice here :

A woman who appeared as a witness in a case which
Judge Ross was trying wore a huge bonnet that concealed
her countenance. Judge Ross asked her to remove her
bonnet. She declined, and when the judge asked her rea-
sons she declared she had the authority of Scripture,
which admonished women to remain covered in public
assemblages. Judge Ross commended her for her wis-
dom. "You ought to be on the bench," he concluded.
"No, thank you, Judge," replied the woman. "There are
already enough old women on the bench."

As two of the old-time associate judges not learned
in the law were sitting with Judge Ross, perhaps her
comment was not leveled wholly at the president judge.

His idiosyncrasies, together with his failing health,
engendered rumors that Judge Ross was suffering from
a mental affliction shortly after he entered upon his
duties as a justice of the Supreme Court. A petition was
presented to the State Legislature asking that he be removed because of mental incompetence. The Legislature

appointed a committee to investigate. When the committee heard witnesses, Judge Ross cross-examined the witnesses so effectively that the committee decided it was unnecessary for witnesses on behalf of the judge to appear, and the petition was dismissed.

His health nevertheless was seriously affected, and he could give but limited attention to his duties in the Supreme Court. He died in Philadelphia in 1834, at the age of 64.

Many years before, while living in Easton, Judge Ross had bought several hundred acres of wild land amidst the foothills of the Blue Mountains, near Wind Gap. He called the locality Ross Common. Some members of the family lived there, at least in the summertime. At Ross Common Judge Ross set apart a family burial ground, and therein he was buried. The locality, now in Monroe county, is today known as Ross Township.

After Judge Ross' death his widow lived at Jenkintown. She exerted herself in the endeavor to further the progress of the community. The site on which the attractive little building of the Jenkintown Lyceum was erected, was a gift from her, and until it was ready for occupancy, the Lyceum met at her home. Indeed, her activity in this organization nearly split it because certain members believed women should be seen but not heard. The old Lyceum building is now occupied by the Abington Library. Mrs. Ross died in 1846.

Two sons of Judge Ross, Thomas and George, both became members of the Bucks county bar. Thomas was long a leader in politics. When but 24 years old he was appointed deputy attorney general for Bucks county. In those days the attorney general of the state appointed deputies to attend to the duties now assigned to the district attorneys. Later Thomas Ross served two terms in Congress.

George Ross disappeared under strange circumstances. He had a controversy with another young man about a girl of whom both were enamored. They decided to settle the dispute by fighting a duel with pistols. But instead of going somewhere into the woods to fight it out, this duel was fought in a boat on the Delaware River. After the duel George Ross was never again seen by his family or friends. Whether he was killed or decided to leave the locality never was ascertained.

Two sons of Thomas Ross gained eminence in politics and the law. Henry P. Ross followed in the footsteps of his grandfather by becoming president judge of Montgomery county. George Ross, his brother, was a member of the State Constitutional Convention of 1873, a member of the State Senate for two terms and Democratic candidate for United States Senator against Matthew S. Quay. Two sons of George Ross maintained the legal prestige of the family by practicing law in Doylestown.

JOHN FOX

UPON the advancement of Judge John Ross to the Supreme Court of Pennsylvania, John Fox, of Bucks county, was appointed president judge in the Bucks-Montgomery judicial district.

Judge Fox some years before that had been called the "dictator general of the Democratic party." Unquestionably he was a powerful influence in the politics of his day. Though his health was never robust, whatever duties he undertook, whether at the bar, in politics, or in public office, he pursued with intense zeal and earnestness.

When the county seat of Bucks county was moved from Newtown to Doylestown, in 1813, John Fox was one of the eight lawyers comprising the bar of the county who also moved from Newtown to Doylestown. He was then 26 years old. He had been born in Philadelphia, where his father, Edward Fox, had been auditor general of Pennsylvania, and later was treasurer of the University of Pennsylvania. The son studied law with Alexander J. Dallas, afterwards secretary of the treasury, a fellow-student having been Mr. Dallas' son, George M. Dallas, who subsequently became the Vice President of the United States. At the advice of his physician John Fox decided to take up the practice of law in a rural district, and so made his home in Newtown.

The year after moving to Doylestown John Fox was appointed deputy attorney general for Bucks county, an office corresponding to the district attorney of today. Serving in that capacity, ere long he had a collision with the scruples of Judge Bird Wilson. When the British captured Washington in 1814 and threatened Philadelphia great alarm ensued throughout southeastern Pennsylvania. Notwithstanding physical disabilities John Fox volunteered his services and became a member of General Worrall's staff.   Court convened in Doylestown at the height of the excitement.   Fox, as public prosecutor, alluded to the menace of war threatening Pennsylvania and asked that court be adjourned so that anyone interested in the cases to be heard might join the army.   Judge Wilson declined to comply with the request.   Thereupon Fox continued all the cases until the next term, strode out of the court room and left the court without any work to do.

Besides holding the rank of major on the staff of General Worrall in the War of 1812, John Fox was later appointed major general of the Seventh Division of Pennsylvania Militia, but he did not take up his commission for that post.

He received the appointment of president judge of the Bucks-Montgomery district in 1830.   Two years later he presided at one of the most notable trials in the history of Bucks county, when a Spaniard named Mina was accused of the murder of Dr. William Chapman, of Bensalem township.   Dr. Chapman was widely known as the discoverer of a cure for stammering.

Mina came to the Chapman home one day in June, 1831, and asked permission to stay over night.   He remained some time and apparently Mrs. Chapman became infatuated with him.   In a few days Dr. Chapman died and Mina left the house.   Some months later he was arrested in Boston and brought to Doylestown. He and Mrs. Chapman were charged with the murder of Dr. Chapman by poisoning him.

While awaiting trial Mina escaped from the Doylestown prison by burning a hole in the floor of his cell.   He was soon recaptured in Hilltown township.

Mrs. Chapman was tried before Judge Fox in February, 1832, the proceedings continuing five days. During this time Judge Fox ordered the newspapers not to print anything relating to the trial.   The jury acquitted Mrs. Chapman.

Mina's trial followed in April. He was found guilty. When he was hanged, six weeks later, on the grounds of the Bucks County Almshouse, the occasion was made a gala day for Bucks county, all the militia companies of the county turning out and thousands of people witnessing the execution of the death sentence.

The decision of Judge Fox in another case had far-reaching import. It concerned the right of a free negro to vote. Judge Fox ruled that the negro was not entitled to the franchise. The opinion was quoted by DeTocqueville in his noted work, "Democracy in America," and it is said to have brought about the inclusion of the word "white," limiting the right of suffrage, in the state constitution of 1838.

This same new constitution of 1838 indirectly cost Judge Fox his office of president judge. Up to that time president judges were appointed for life by the governor of the state. Among the citizens a strong feeling had prevailed ever since the time of the Revolution that the courts ought to be democratized and that judges were assuming too much authority. In line with this tendency of thought the constitution of 1838 deprived judges of the life right to their positions which they then held and made their term of office ten years.

Consequently Judge Fox's term ended in 1840. Governor David R. Porter nominated Judge Fox for another term. Such nominations had to be submitted to the State Senate for approval. In the Senate a long controversy ensued over the nomination. Judge Fox's political foes, who were numerous, set about to encompass his defeat. Members of the bar presented a protest against his reappointment, setting forth that while his legal ability was unquestioned he was not an ideal judge because of his personal bias and his irascibility.

Petitions opposing his confirmation were circulated. It was said that in Bucks county an arrangement was made with a man to obtain signatures to the petitions at 10 cents a head. The list thus accumulated was so long that it constituted a severe drain upon the treasury of Judge Fox's opponents. Later it was asserted that many of the names were copied from gravestones or were otherwise bogus. At any rate the fight against Judge Fox brought about the withdrawal of his name, Governor Porter appointing Judge Thomas Burnside, of Center county, instead.

On another occasion the political animosity against Judge Fox caused some of his enemies to elect him to the office of constable in Doylestown. Instead of showing annoyance, however, he accepted the office and performed its duties.

He was the close friend of Samuel D. Ingham, of Bucks county, who became secretary of the treasury under President Jackson. Many an important political move was determined by these two men. Judge Fox also maintained a correspondence for many years with John C. Calhoun, the noted Southern leader of the Democratic party.

Judge Fox's wife was Margery, daughter of Gilbert Rodman, a Philadelphia merchant. Their three sons all entered the bar, but one of them, Lewis R. Fox, later became a Presbyterian minister, while Gilbert Rodman Fox and Edward J. Fox continued to practice law. Gilbert Rodman Fox made his home in Norristown, where he was one of the leading lawyers up to his death, in 1892. His son, Gilbert Rodman Fox, has been a member of the Montgomery county bar since 1885.

Judge Fox, on leaving the bench, continued to practice law in Doylestown until his death, in 1849.

THOMAS BURNSIDE

AS a judge, Thomas Burnside had a career that was much more varied and picturesque than that of the average jurist. He served in three different judicial districts of Pennsylvania and closed his career as a justice of the Supreme Court of the state.

When the fight over the reappointment of Judge John Fox in the Bucks-Montgomery judicial district developed in the State Senate, in 1840, Governor David R. Porter remembered the capable services which his long-time friend, Thomas Burnside, had been giving ever since 1826 in the district of which Center county was a part, and to avoid becoming entangled in the political quarrels of Bucks and Montgomery counties, the governor transferred Judge Burnside to the post which Judge Fox was vacating.

The Porters and the Burnsides had become acquainted in the previous generation when both families lived in Norriton township, Montgomery county. Both were of Scotch-Irish lineage, and both were members of the old Norriton Presbyterian church, on the Germantown pike.

William Burnside and his family came to Montgomery county in 1792 from County Tyrone, Ireland. The son Thomas was then 10 years old. First they lived for a short time on Egypt road, now Main street, Norristown, near Stony Creek. Then they moved to the neighborhood of the Norriton church.

About the father there are traditions that he was one of the last to cling to the costume of the eighteenth century, including buckskin breeches, long stockings, a cocked hat and silver shoe buckles.

It is said the son Thomas began reading law books while confined to his room with a broken leg, the injury having been received when he was thrown from a horse.

He continued his legal studies with Robert Porter, in Philadelphia. Shortly after being admitted to the bar, in 1804, he took up his residence in Bellefonte, Center county, then virtually a frontier town.

Though unacquainted and without financial means, his ability and popularity won him political recognition. In 1811 he was elected to the State Senate, and three years later he was sent to Congress. While still a member of Congress Governor Snyder appointed him president judge of the Luzerne district. But he resigned this office in 1818 and resumed the practice of law in Bellefonte.

He was again elected to the State Senate in 1823 and was made speaker of the Senate. In 1826 he was appointed president judge of the Center county district, and he held that post until Governor Porter sent him to the Bucks-Montgomery district, in 1841.

The opponents of long terms of service in the judiciary let themselves be heard when Judge Burnside's nomination came before the State Senate. Six senators made speeches against the confirmation of the nomination, largely because they held he had been a judge long enough. However, he won by a majority of seven votes.

Many anecdotes told about Judge Burnside concern his unprepossessing personal appearance. In jovial mood he would often claim the distinction of being the homeliest man in the state. When he came to the Bucks-Montgomery district, however, he contended that in the matter of homely features he had a worthy rival in his predecessor, Judge Fox.

His indifference to dress accentuated the effect produced by his face, and it was said he delighted to pose as a tramp. When he arrived at the home where he was to stay in Doylestown, the woman of the house, alarmed by the appearance of the stranger, sent in haste for her husband. From him she was astounded to learn that the visitor was the new judge.

But his knowledge of the law was thorough, and he was a good judge. Sometimes, perhaps, he had orig-

inal ways of construing evidence, as on one occasion
when several men were convicted before him for riot-
ing along the canal in the central part of the state.
When one of the culprits was called for sentence, his
attorney urged that the evidence showed this man was
not near the scene of the disorder but was on the opposite side of the river. "That may be," replied Judge
Burnside, "yet from what I know about him I feel
sure that if he could have got across he would have
been in it." So he proceeded to impose sentence.

When appointed to the Center county bench Judge
Burnside succeeded Judge Huston, who was advanced
to the Supreme Court. By the operation of the constitution of 1838 Judge Huston's Supreme Court term
expired in 1845. Governor Porter then named Judge
Burnside for this post, and the Senate confirmed the
nomination.

He remained on the Supreme Court bench until
his death, which occurred at the home of his son-in-
law, William E. Morris, in Germantown, March 25,
1851.

His son James, who married a daughter of Simon
Cameron, also became a lawyer and a judge, being
appointed president judge of the Center county district in 1853. He was killed by being thrown from his
carriage, in Bellefonte, in 1859.

DAVID KRAUSE

MORE than any of his predecessors as president judge of the Montgomery county courts, Judge David Krause, who assumed the bench in 1845, made himself one of the community in Norristown and entered enthusiastically into the civic and political activities of the town. He served but six years as president judge, but he remained a resident of Norristown to the end of his life, twenty years later, and during that period he was honored and respected as the spokesman for the people of the borough in many an important endeavor, notably during the trying times of the Civil War.

Judge Krause was practicing law in Harrisburg when Governor Porter, toward the end of his term of office, appointed him president judge of the Bucks-Montgomery district, to fill the vacancy due to the advancement of Judge Thomas Burnside to the Supreme Court.

Before coming to Norristown Judge Krause had been the close friend of a succession of Pennsylvania's governors. He was a native of Lebanon county, whence came John Andrew Shulze, the Lutheran minister who forsook the pulpit to take up politics and was elected governor of the state in 1823. David Krause, then 23 years old, was practicing law in Lebanon. He gave his whole-hearted support to Shulze's candidacy. When Shulze went to Harrisburg as governor he took Krause with him as his secretary.

At the time of General Lafayette's visit to the United States, in 1824, David Krause probably visited Norristown for the first time. He accompanied Governor Shulze to Philadelphia to greet Lafayette. The officials made the journey in coaches, and were accompanied by the Dauphin Cavalry. They arrived in Nor-

ristown toward evening on Saturday, September 18.
The governor being opposed to Sunday travel, he and
his retinue remained in Norristown until Monday, the
governor being the guest of Philip S. Markley, then a
member of Congress.   Sunday morning Governor
Shulze and his secretary attended services in the Presbyterian church, and in the afternoon at the Episcopal
church.

At this period Mr. Krause made the acquaintance
of Simon Cameron, who was then launching forth on
his career as a political leader.   They remained life-
long friends.   For a time they were associated in the
publication of the Pennsylvania Intelligencer, which
was the state organ of the Democratic Party.

For one year Mr. Krause was deputy attorney
general for Dauphin county.   In 1835 he was elected
to the State House of Representatives as a Whig.   Once
more he took up editorial work, on the State Journal.
But the practice of law in Harrisburg was his chief
occupation.

He took his seat as president judge of the Bucks-
Montgomery district on September 17, 1845, making
his home in Norristown.

His career on the bench was marked by few attempts at elaboration in legal discussion.   His opinions
were uniformly brief and concise, yet covering all the
matters at issue.

Like nearly all other judges in the state, Judge
Krause was strongly opposed to an elective judiciary.
When his term ended, in 1851, the voters were for the
first time to elect the president judge of the district.
This was another step in the struggle that had been in
progress ever since the time of the Revolution to limit
the powers of the judiciary.   First the judges were
appointed for life.   Then, by the constitution of 1838,
their term was fixed at ten years, though they could
be reappointed.   Now an amendment to the state constitution called for the election of judges by the people.

Almost unanimously the judges raised their voices
against what they regarded as a lowering of the dig-

nity of their office. To subject the judiciary to the vicissitudes of politics was degrading in the extreme, declared the judges. On hearing the news of the adoption of the amendment Justice Thomas Burnside, of the State Supreme Court, who had preceded Judge Krause on the bench of the Bucks-Montgomery district, remarked that it would not be long now before Joe Barker would be elected chief justice. Joe Barker, a labor agitator, had just been sent to jail for inciting a riot in Allegheny City.

Judge Krause evidenced the conscientiousness of his objections to the new regulations by refusing to be a candidate for election to the office which he held, though he could have had the nomination. David M. Smyser was elected president judge, and Judge Krause retired from office and took up the practice of law in the courts over which he had presided.

While he was yet on the bench the feeling over the slavery issue was assuming a dangerous aspect, even here in Montgomery county. The court house— the old building erected in the eighteenth century and standing south of Penn street in what is now the public Square—was the only auditorium in the town available for political meetings. There the Democrats, who opposed interference with slavery, and the Whigs, who resisted the spread of slavery in new states, alternately held meetings, and occasionally the radicals who sought to wipe out slavery altogether also assembled there to listen to Rev. Samuel Aaron or some other noted abolition orator.

Once it happened that the official responsible for giving permission to use the court house for public meetings confused his dates and authorized both the Whigs and the Democrats to meet in the court house on the same night. The leaders of the two parties agreed to endeavor to prevent trouble by holding the two meetings in succession, the Whigs meeting first. But when the time came for the Whigs to vacate they "held the fort," refusing to admit the Democrats. The lights were turned out and a free-for-all fight began.

The town's constables were summoned, but they were helpless. Then Judge Krause was notified. Some lights were procured, and Judge Krause mounted the bench. He sternly commanded that the court room be cleared. His determined attitude was effective and the commotion ended.

When no longer bound by the rules of judicial impartiality, Judge Krause threw the weight of his influence in behalf of the foes of slavery, and he was one of the principal speakers for the newly organized Republican party.

When the Civil War opened, in 1861, he spoke at all the patriotic meetings held to encourage enlistment of troops. Though he was 62 years old he joined the emergency troops in 1862 and was in the field for two weeks. Again in 1863, when the Southern army invaded Pennsylvania, Judge Krause enlisted as a private in the Forty-third Regiment, and for six weeks he followed the daily duties of the soldier in guarding mills along the Potomac.

Judge Krause was made the Republican candidate for Congress in 1862, but as Democratic control of the district had been assured by attaching Lehigh county to Montgomery, there was no chance for his election. However, he enthusiastically stumped the district during the campaign.

His death occurred June 13, 1871, and he was buried in Montgomery cemetery, Norristown. One of those who attended the funeral was Simon Cameron.

In 1829 Judge Krause married Catharine Orr, of Philadelphia. Their daughter Mary became the wife of Dr. Mahlon Preston, long a leading homeopathic practitioner in Norristown.

DANIEL M. SMYSER

DANIEL M. SMYSER, who became president judge of the Bucks-Montgomery district in 1851, was the first president judge elected by the voters of the district. Prior to that time appointments were made first by the Supreme Executive Council of the state and then by the governor. An amendment to the state constitution adopted in 1850 made the office elective.

Though the Democratic Party was dominant in the district, it lost the opportunity to place a lawyer of that political faith on the bench. The Bucks county Democratic convention named Henry Chapman, of Doylestown, for judge. The Montgomery county Democratic convention proposed Joseph Fornance, of Norristown. Four conferees from each county met at Montgomery Square to decide upon the nominee. The conference was opened on Monday and continued until midnight on Saturday. Ballot after ballot was taken, the result always standing four for Chapman and four for Fornance.

As the deadlock could not be broken, both of the candidates went before the voters at the election.

The Whigs wanted Judge David Krause to run as their candidate, but his opposition to an elective judiciary caused him to decline to be a candidate to succeed himself. Thereupon the Whigs took up Daniel M. Smyser, a Gettysburg lawyer, as their candidate. His election followed.

Thus, as in the case of Judge Krause and Judge Burnside, a man was brought here from a distance to preside over the courts. Such a course was frequently deemed desirable in the interests of fairness, it being assumed that a judge who was not under any kind of local obligations would be better fitted to serve with impartiality.

Page fifty-three

Judge Smyser was 42 years old when he ascended the bench. He had studied law in Gettysburg with Thaddeus Stevens and was his law partner until Stevens moved to Lancaster, in 1842.

As a member of the State House of Representatives, to which he was elected in 1849, Mr. Smyser proved himself an able debater. Recognizing his ability, Governor William F. Johnston appointed Smyser attorney general. He declined to accept the office, however, on the ground that he was bound to serve out the term in the Legislature for which he was elected.

The nomination for judge of the Bucks-Montgomery district came to him without any previous consultation on the subject. He accepted the nomination, and when elected he made his home in Norristown.

In the fifties, while Judge Smyser was on the bench, Montgomery county finally determined to abandon the old court house and county office building which had been erected in the preceding century, upon the establishment of the county. An extensive building program was undertaken, covering several years. First the old prison, at Swede and Airy streets, was removed, and then a splendid marble court house was erected, facing Swede street, the grounds occupying the block from Swede to Penn street. The old buildings, south of Penn street, were removed, and the site became part of the Public Square.

When completed, the new court house, which cost $150,000, was declared to be the handsomest building of its kind in the state. It was opened in 1854, and Judge Smyser was the first judge to hold court in it.

One of the most important cases adjudicated by Judge Smyser involved the right to hold services of the Episcopal faith in Christ (Swedes') church, Upper Merion. As early as 1848 certain members of that church had applied to the court for an injunction against Episcopal services, contending that this was established as a Lutheran church and the congregation had never become part of the Protestant Episcopal denomination. Judge Krause, who was then on the bench, dismissed the equity suit of 1848.

In 1853 the litigation was reopened before Judge Smyser. As was his custom he went into the matters in controversy with extreme care and thoroughness. His opinion as rendered comprised about 10,000 words, reviewing the historical, theological and legal aspects of the dispute.

He explained there were various forms of Lutheranism, and the Swedish Lutheran church was akin to the Protestant Episcopal church in that both recognized the episcopacy and both used vestments and the liturgy in their services.

It had been alleged that the Episcopal church was Calvanistic and predestinarian, thus differing radically from the Lutheran faith. This question, too, was considered at length in the opinion. Whatever dogmatic differences might be found, Judge Smyser held that as the services of the Episcopal clergymen had been accepted without protest at Swedes' church since the beginning of the century, the members of 1853 possessed no right in equity to object, and the suit was therefore dismissed.

Judge Smyser was solicitous about the welfare of the younger members of the bar to a marked degree. To afford them practice in legal procedure a moot court was organized, over which Judge Smyser himself presided. For several years, from November until April, the moot court met every Monday night in a room in the court house, and Judge Smyser gave the same careful attention to the imaginary suits thus tried that he did to the actual litigation which came before him.

In 1854 Judge Smyser was the Whig nominee for judge of the Supreme Court, opposing Chief Justice Black, but he went down to defeat with his party.

When Judge Smyser's ten-year term expired, in 1861, the Democrats were united and had no difficulty in electing their candidate, Henry Chapman, of Bucks county.

On retiring from the bench, Judge Smyser continued to live in Norristown, and for years he was frequently called upon to speak at important political and patriotic assemblages.

He died January 13, 1873, while on a visit to his son-in-law, David Wills, in Gettysburg. A year later David Wills became president judge of the Forty-second Judicial District.

HENRY CHAPMAN

IN the sense that "no news is good news," the services of Henry Chapman as president judge of the Bucks-Montgomery judicial district, from 1861 until 1871, were all that are to be expected from a capable jurist. Few troublesome legal problems required his attention and few unusual criminal trials took place. Judge Chapman was a man of legal erudition and wide general culture, but he did not do extraordinary things such as create anecdotes and legend.

This is said of him, however: That his conception of the honor due his office was of so lofty a standard that he declined to accept passes from railroads at a time when such passes were distributed with great generosity and that he even refused to ride in the private conveyances of lawyers practicing in his courts.

He was the son of Abraham Chapman, who had been a member of the Bucks county bar since 1790 and in his later years was known as the "father" of the bar of his county. The son Henry was born in Wrightstown, Bucks county, in 1801, but was reared in Doylestown and lived there all his life. Upon becoming a member of the bar he succeeded to the lucrative practice of his father.

His activity in the Democratic Party brought about Henry Chapman's nomination for the State Senate in 1843, his election resulting.

In 1847 Governor William F. Johnston appointed Mr. Chapman president judge of the judicial district comprising Chester and Delaware counties. He held that office for four years. Then, in 1851, the Bucks County Democratic convention indorsed him as candidate for president judge of the Bucks-Montgomery district, the first election of a judge taking place that year under an amendment of the state constitution.

A Democratic nomination was equivalent usually to an election in those days. Preferring to serve in his home district rather than in the Chester-Delaware district, Judge Chapman declined the nomination which was offered him in the latter district and became a candidate in the Bucks-Montgomery district.

But the Montgomery county Democrats, also relying upon the impregnable position of their party, insisted upon having the candidate for judge, their choice being Joseph Fornance of Norristown. The conference of the two counties remained deadlocked for a week. A choice apparently being impossible, both Mr. Chapman and Mr. Fornance remained in the field as candidates. Taking advantage of the split the Whigs elected their nominee, Daniel M. Smyser, of Gettysburg.

Judge Chapman now resumed the practice of law in Doylestown. In 1856 he was elected to the National House of Representatives, and served one term there.

When Judge Smyser's term expired, in 1861, the Montgomery county Democrats yielded to their political associates in the other county of the judicial district, with the result that now Mr. Chapman was elected judge. He continued to live in Doylestown during his term of office.

Wartime conditions affected litigation. With so many men in the army and with public attention focused on the progress of the war, work for the courts was diminished.

The most notable criminal trial during Judge Chapman's incumbency was that of Jacob Hodapp, charged with the murder of Julius Wochele. Wochele, a recently arrived German immigrant, was found slain one morning in November, 1865, in the barnyard of an untenanted farm on the Bethlehem pike, near Montgomery Square, he having apparently been beaten to death. He had been boarding in Philadelphia, and Hodapp, a fellow boarder, disappeared about the time that Wochele was killed.

No light was shed on the crime until the following May, when the consul of Wurtemburg, in Philadelphia, received a draft for $40 intended for Wochele, the accompanying letter explaining that the money, from the estate of his parents in Germany, was forwarded in accordance with Wochele's request. An address was given, to which the consul sent the draft. A receipt was returned from Allentown. There police found Hodapp and arrested him.

It transpired that Hodapp had learned from Wochele about the money due him from his parents' estate, had lured him out to the untenanted farm on Bethlehem pike, where Hodapp formerly worked, and there had killed Wochele, afterwards personating him in letters sent to Germany appealing for financial aid.

Hodapp was tried before Judge Chapman in Norristown in November, 1866, and was convicted of murder in the first degree. He was hanged on February 6, 1867.

Upon the expiration of his term as president judge, in 1871, Judge Chapman declined to be a candidate for re-election. He resumed the practice of law in Doylestown. His death occurred April 11, 1891.

Judge Chapman's first wife was Rebecca Stewart. Later he married Nancy Findlay Shunk, a daughter of Governor Francis R. Shunk, of Trappe.

HENRY P. ROSS

TOWARD the end of Judge Henry Chapman's term as president judge of the Bucks-Montgomery district it was evident that the business requiring the attention of the courts was more than one judge could well conduct, even though he had the assistance in much of the detail of two associate judges not learned in the law. A movement was started to have the Legislature authorize the appointment of an additional law judge for the district. It was successful, and in 1869, Henry Pawling Ross, of Doylestown, was named to fill that office.

Upon the expiration of Judge Chapman's term, in 1871, he declined to seek re-election. Judge Ross was then made the Democratic candidate for president judge, and his election for the full ten-year term followed.

Thus Judge Ross succeeded to the office which his grandfather, Judge John Ross had filled, from 1818 until 1830. He made his home in Norristown, with which community he was already well acquainted. His mother, the wife of Thomas Ross, was the eldest daughter of Levi Pawling, long one of the foremost citizens of Norristown, burgess for several terms, director of the Bank of Montgomery County, member of Congress and owner of much real estate.

For three years Judge Ross continued as head of the courts in the two counties constituting the district, but he usually gave most of his attention to the Montgomery county courts, while the additional law judge presided in the Doylestown courts. Following Judge Ross' resignation as additional law judge when he became president judge, Arthur G. Olmstead, of Bucks county, was named for the office. He held court only one term, and then resigned because of ill health. His

successor was Stokes L. Roberts, also of Bucks county.
He, too, found the duties of the office uncongenial because of failing health, and he soon resigned. Then
the office was given to Richard Watson, another Bucks
county lawyer.

By an enactment of the State Legislature in 1874
the judicial district was divided into two districts,
Bucks and Montgomery county each constituting a
district. Judge Ross remained in Montgomery county
as president judge.

Like numerous other members of the Ross family,
Judge Ross was keenly interested in the maneuverings
of politics. In 1862, three years after having been
admitted to the bar, he was elected district attorney of
Bucks county. He was the Democratic nominee for
Congress in 1864 and 1866, but was defeated both times.
He attended the Democratic National Convention as a
delegate in 1864 and 1868.

While judge he was proposed for the Democratic
nomination for Governor, and in 1876 nearly won that
distinçtion in the state convention. Two years later
he was made the Democratic nominee for judge of the
Supreme Court, but he failed of election.

Judge Ross' term was notable for several unusual
murder trials that attracted much attention. Two of
these took place in 1875.

Thomas Francis Curley was convicted of murdering Mary Ann Whitby, near Trappe. He was hanged.

Blasius Pistorius was on trial for four days on the
charge of having shot and killed Isaac Jaquett, on a
farm along Stony Creek, where Elmwood Park now is.
The two men lived on adjoining properties, and a controversy over boundary lines had developed, leading to
a quarrel and the shooting. Judge Ross pronounced
the death sentence on Pistorius at midnight, following
the jury's verdict that the prisoner was guilty. However, the sentence was not executed, as Pistorius became a raving maniac, and died shortly afterward in
the State Hospital for the Insane.

In 1877 there was the trial of Henri Wahlen,

accused of killing Max Hugo Hoehne, at Elm Station, now Narberth. For a long time after the dead body was found it was not identified. A group of Lower Merion citizens employed a detective to make an investigation. After sending some of the clothing, together with a photograph of the corpse, to Germany, Hoehne was identified. Later Hoehne's father received a letter purporting to come from his son and asking for money. Through this letter Wahlen was arrested in Brooklyn. So well was the circumstantial evidence marshaled that Wahlen was convicted of murder in the first degree.

Wahlen cheated the gallows by battering out his brains in his cell in the Montgomery county prison.

At the election in 1881 Judge Ross was the Democratic candidate to succeed himself. The Republicans nominated Aaron S. Swartz. Judge Ross won by a majority of 1126 votes.

But Judge Ross lived to serve only a brief fraction of his second term. He died after a few days' illness on Thursday, April 13, 1882. The previous Monday he had held court, but he gave evidence then of feebleness. For some time he had been suffering from a rheumatic affliction that made it almost impossible for him to write. He was but 46 years old.

The funeral was held from his home, on Swede street, above Airy, and burial followed in Doylestown, the entire membership of the bar accompanying the body on a train on the Stony Creek Railroad.

By his will Judge Ross bequeathed his gold-headed cane and his set of "State Trials" to Harman Yerkes, described as "my old and favorite student," who was appointed executor and trustee under the will. The "favorite student" followed in the judicial footsteps of his preceptor, serving long and capably as president judge of Bucks county.

Judge Ross was married in 1865 to Mary Clifton, of Princeton, N. J. She died in 1873, one daughter surviving. In 1875 Judge Ross married Emily Genung, of Brooklyn.

Associate Judges
Not Versed In The Law

TO the present generation it seems almost fantastic that as late as 1876 judges who had not studied the law sat upon the bench of Montgomery county. Yet it was not until the present constitution of Pennsylvania went into effect, in 1874, that all judges were required to be learned in the law.

It has already been related that in early years strong feeling existed among the people of the state against giving lawyers too much power in court proceedings. Until the constitution of 1790 was adopted, the county judges were the justices of the peace. Thereafter the president judge had to be a lawyer. In addition each county had three or four associate judges, of whom knowledge of the law was not required. Subsequently a change was made making the number of associate judges two in each county.

Moreover, these lay judges possessed real power. The two of them united could overrule the president judge, not only in questions of fact but also of law. At least one associate judge had to be on the bench in order to constitute court. Usually, though, the president judge was tactful enough to endeavor to win the lay judges to his view of the case, so that disagreements were not frequent.

An interesting case tried in the fifties, with Judge Smyser presiding, resulted in a disagreement between the president judge and his two associates, the issue being whether or not fraud entered into a real estate transaction. In announcing the decision of the bench Judge Smyser had to admit he was overruled by his two associates. The case was appealed to the Supreme Court, where the decision of the associate judges was sustained.

Under certain circumstances an associate judge could act alone. Several cases centering about attempts to capture fugitive slaves, which caused much excitement at the time, were decided by associate judges.

In February, 1829, John Lewis, a negro in the employ of Peter Dager, in Whitemarsh township, was arrested charged with being a fugitive slave. He had escaped from his owner, near Harper's Ferry, Va., three years before, along with a brother and two other negroes. Lewis fought his captors, but was overpowered and placed in a wagon. About the same time his brother was also caught. The captors were on their way to Philadelphia with the two negroes, when Peter Dager overtook them at Barren Hill and compelled them to bring the negroes to Norristown to have the matter investigated in court.

Great indignation was aroused in the community, for Lewis had made many friends. Prominent residents of Whitemarsh and Plymouth came to Norristown, when the case was heard by Associate Judge Richard B. Jones, without a jury. Four witnesses identified the negroes as escaped slaves. It transpired that another negro had betrayed them to win a reward.

Judge Jones ordered that the two prisoners be returned to Virginia. The Whitemarsh people resolved this should not be done. They made overtures to the owner of the negroes, with the result that he agreed to release his claims on payment of $600 for John Lewis and $300 for the brother. Peter Dager paid the $600 and Ezra Comfort the $300. The negroes made their home at Spring Mill and repaid the two men who had secured their freedom.

In 1823 a fugitive negro was caught in Horsham township. Citizens of Horsham caused the arrest of five men implicated in the capture on a charge of kidnapping. The jury in the kidnapping case acquitted the men. Judge Ross, who presided, placed the negro in jail to await a hearing. That was on Saturday. On Monday, before either Judge Ross or Associate

Judge McNeill had arrived in Norristown, Associate Judge Richard B. Jones gave the claimants an order permitting them to take the negro away with them. Subsequently the men arrested for kidnapping sued their prosecutors and won an award of $4000 damages against five of them.

Associate judges, like the president judges, were appointed by the governor until by an amendment to the constitution the office of judge was made elective. But instead of a ten-year term, as was given to the president judges, the associate judges' terms were five years.

Numerous well known men of the county served as associate judges. The first group appointed under the constitution of 1790 consisted of Samuel Potts, Benjamin Rittenhouse, Robert Loller and Benjamin Markley.

Benjamin Rittenhouse was a brother of the famous scientist and statesman, David Rittenhouse. It was he who made most of the so-called Rittenhouse clocks now in existence. At the time of the Revolution he was superintendent of the governmental gunlock factory in Philadelphia.

Robert Loller was a patriot of the Revolution who subsequently held numerous public offices and who by his will founded Loller Academy, in Hatboro.

Joseph Royer, of Trappe, whom Governor Ritner appointed in 1837, had served in the State Legislature and was prominent in politics. Two of his sons, Horace and Lewis, subsequently were members of the State Senate.

Josiah W. Evans, who became an associate judge in 1843, was reappointed in 1848 and elected in 1851, is a type of the average associate judge of the nineteenth century. He was a native of Limerick township. His only education consisted of what he acquired in the short winter terms of the township schools. He learned the trade of blacksmith, and then went to farming, but in 1831 Jacob Fry, Sr., prothonotary of the county, appointed Mr. Evans as his clerk. From thence on he lived in Norristown, serving a term as prothonotary before being appointed associate judge. He was also a member of the School Board and of Town Council, being clerk of council for a time.

Henry Longaker also was a good example of the kind of men who sat on the bench. He was a Mennonite farmer who, after tilling different farms in Upper and Lower Providence township, became proprietor of the Perkiomen Bridge Hotel. He was elected justice of the peace, sheriff and member of the State House of Representatives. He was associate judge for two terms, from 1851 until 1861.

Others who held this office, with the dates of their appointment or election, were: John Jones, 1793; Richard B. Jones, 1822; Thomas Lowry, 1824; Morris Longstreth, 1841; Ephraim Fenton, 1848; Joseph Hunsicker, 1849; Nathaniel Jacoby, 1855; John Dismant, 1861; Hiram C. Hoover, 1870; Isaac F. Yost, 1871.

Judge Jacoby, who held the office for two terms, was librarian of the Law Library in the court house in his later years.

Hiram C. Hoover, who became widely known through the reunions of the Hoover family, of which he was president for many years, was a storekeeper and farmer at Hooverton, on the Germantown pike, north of Stony Creek. He lived until 1911, attaining the age of 89 years.

The last of the associate judges to sit on the bench in Montgomery county was Judge Isaac F. Yost, elected in 1871. The constitution of 1874 abolished the office but permitted the judges then sitting to complete their terms. When Judge Yost performed the duties of his office for the last time, on November 10, 1876, the members of the bar assembled to accord him a parting tribute. Judge Ross spoke of the integrity and honesty of his retiring associate, and B. Markley Boyer and Colonel Theodore W. Bean voiced the high regard that the lawyers had for Judge Yost.

From that time on Judge Ross and after him Judge Boyer alone conducted the court proceedings of the county until 1887, when the Legislature created the office of additional law judge for Montgomery county and Aaron S. Swartz was appointed to fill it.

CHARLES H. STINSON

POLITICAL conditions made the term of Charles H. Stinson as president judge of Montgomery county the briefest in the history of the judicial district.

He received the appointment as president judge from Governor Hoyt upon the death of Judge Henry P. Ross, in April, 1882. A few months later the Republican County Convention nominated him for the office he was filling. The Democratic Convention named B. Markley Boyer.

Up to the seventies Montgomery was a Democratic county. In the early eighties the Republicans were in the ascendency. General Garfield, their Presidential nominee, carried the county by one vote, in 1880, over General Hancock, notwithstanding the latter was a native of the county. But in 1882 a strong revolt occurred among the independent Republicans of the state. They nominated John Stewart for governor against General James A. Beaver, the regular Republican nominee. The issue was vigorously fought in every county of the state, and the outcome was to the pronounced advantage of the Democrats. Their candidate for governor, Robert E. Pattison, was elected, as were many local candidates of the party.

Incidental to this campaign Judge Stinson lost his office, Mr. Boyer being elected and assuming the bench at the opening of 1883.

During his brief service Judge Stinson gave ample evidence of his qualifications for the duties of the office.

Eleven years earlier Judge Stinson had had an opportunity to go upon the bench. Then the district still consisted of the two counties, Bucks and Montgomery. An additional law judge was authorized for the district in 1869, Henry P. Ross, of Doylestown, being appointed. Upon the retirement of Judge Chapman, in 1871, Judge Ross was elected president judge. Governor Geary then offered Mr. Stinson the position of additional law judge, but he declined it.

Judge Stinson was well known in Harrisburg and among state officials of that period by reason of the fact that for two terms, in 1869 and 1870, he was speaker of the State Senate. He had been elected to the State Senate in 1867, as the Republican nominee. The district comprised Montgomery, Chester and Delaware counties, and although Montgomery county was Democratic the district as a whole was safely Republican.

It is curious that Judge Stinson was the first lawyer regularly engaged in practice in Montgomery county who was appointed or elected to the bench in this county. From 1790, when the state constitution first required the president judge to be learned in the law, up to 1882, every president judge who sat upon the bench in Montgomery county came from some other county, though one of them, Judge Thomas Burnside, was a native of this county.

Like several of his able predecessors, Judge Stinson came from a Scotch-Irish family. His father, Robert Stinson, was a justice of the peace in Norriton township and a member of the State Legislature. Robert Stinson's wife was a niece of General Andrew Porter, of Worcester.

On graduating from Dickinson College, in 1845, Charles H. Stinson studied law in Norristown, first with his brother, George W. Stinson, and after the latter's death with Addison May, being admitted to the bar in 1849.

He was active in the Republican party from its inception in the early fifties. Outside his law practice he was closely identified with three important enterprises of the community.

In 1873 he was one of the leading spirits in organizing the Music Hall Association which built Norristown's first theatre, on the north side of Main street, between DeKalb and Swede streets. He was president of the Hall Association from its origin until his death.

He helped to found the First National Bank of Norristown, in 1864, and was its solicitor for many years, his brother, Francis G. Stinson, being president.

Upon the establishment of the State Hospital in Norristown, in 1879, he was appointed as one of its trustees to represent the commissioners of Montgomery county. He held that office until his death, and was president of the board from 1889 on, having succeeded General John F. Hartranft in that office upon General Hartranft's death.

Largely at the instance of Judge Stinson the women's department of the new hospital was placed in charge of a woman physician. That step was a tremendous innovation at that time. It came about because of the experiences of Judge Stinson's sister, Dr. Mary H. Stinson, in the study of mental ailments.

She was one of the pioneer women physicians of Pennsylvania, having been graduated from the Women's Medical College, Philadelphia, in 1869. She served for five years as a physician in the State Hospital for the Insane, in Worcester, Mass., having been the first woman appointed to such a position. Then she traveled abroad, giving special consideration to methods employed in European institutions for the care of mental patients.

When her brother induced the trustees of the new Norristown State Hospital to consent to the appointment of a woman physician to take charge of the women's department it was natural that the place should be offered to Dr. Stinson. However, she declined it, preferring to live retired in Norristown. She was the founder of the Stinson Home for Aged Women, in Norristown.

After leaving the bench Judge Stinson's law practice was concerned for some years with damage suits arising from the construction of the Pennsylvania Railroad's Schuylkill Valley Branch through Montgomery county, in the eighties, and the building of the same company's Trenton Cut-Off, in the nineties. He represented the railroad company in the litigation, being assisted in many of the suits by his son, C. Henry Stinson, and William F. Solly, who later became judge of the Orphans' Court.

Judge Stinson remained active almost up to the time of his death, which occurred March 10, 1899, at his home, on the west side of Swede street, between Main and Penn. Only a week before his death he presided at a meeting of the State Hospital trustees. He was at that time the last survivor of the trustees appointed when the hospital was established.

NOTWITHSTANDING he was constantly beset by physical handicaps during the period of four and a half years that he was on the bench of Montgomery county, Judge B. Markley Boyer has a conspicuous place in the long line of illustrious judges that have served in this county. Other jurists gave to the public their time and ability which might have won them a rich financial income in the practice of the law. Judge Boyer virtually sacrificed himself in his assiduous attention to the duties of his office.

Afflicted with locomotor ataxia, walking was extremely difficult for him, and he always rode in a carriage between his home, on Sandy street, and the court house. Until within a few months of his death he was the only judge in the county, yet he gave careful attention to the mass of details coming before him in the different courts, his mind remaining clear and vigorous to the last.

Before his election to the judgeship B. Markley Boyer was long one of the outstanding Democrats of the county. In early life he had been a Whig. Twice he was the Whig nominee for State Assembly and once for State Senate, but was defeated each time. In the political campaigns of the forties and early fifties he was often heard on the stump in behalf of the Whig candidates. Henry Clay, General Zachary Taylor and General Winfield Scott all received his ardent support in their presidential campaigns.

But upon the disintegration of the Whig party Mr. Boyer did not follow the general trend of the old-time Whigs toward the new Republican Party. He became a Democrat, and supported the policies of that party in the Civil War era. He was elected to Congress in 1864 and again in 1866.

There were few Democrats in Congress during that reconstruction period, and Mr. Boyer soon gained recognition as one of the ablest representatives of his party. He frequently spoke in Congress against the reconstruction policy of the dominant party, and he was one of the committee appointed on behalf of Congress to investigate the disorders occurring in New Orleans incidental to the efforts of the Federal government to stamp out disloyalty. Following this inquiry Mr. Boyer submitted a minority report to Congress.

Just as he was reluctant to further the movement to free the slaves, so he was disinclined to accept other reform movements of the times. One of the famous controversies of the period preceding the Civil War in Norristown was that conducted in the newspapers of the place between Mr. Boyer and Rev. Samuel Aaron, the fiery leader of all reform movements of that time. In a series of articles manifesting much ability on both sides they debated the pros and cons of slavery, temperance and various other questions.

Notwithstanding his political sympathies, when the Civil War broke out Mr. Boyer was uncompromisingly for the Union, and he proved his sincerity on two occasions by going into service with emergency troops called out when Pennsylvania was threatened with invasion. In 1862 he was captain of a company in the Thirty-first Pennsylvania Militia, which regiment was in the field for two weeks. Charles Hunsicker, later eminent at the Montgomery county bar, was first lieutenant in the same company. In 1863, about the time of the battle of Gettysburg, Mr. Boyer was captain of a company in the 134th Militia. Exposure at that time brought on an attack of typhoid fever.

After the Civil War Mr. Boyer was several times sent as delegate to Democratic National Conventions. He was one of the first to propose the nomination of General Hancock for President. He labored toward that end in 1876, and finally in 1880 his purpose was achieved.

Though of the opposite political faith, Governor John F. Hartranft recognized Mr. Boyer's wide knowledge of civic affairs by appointing him in 1876 as a member of a commission to make a study of the problems of city government and to suggest ways for bringing about improvements, especially in Philadelphia. Much of the research connected with the duties of the commission devolved upon Mr. Boyer, and the break in his health is said to have dated from that period. The outcome of the commission's investigation was the Bullitt Bill, which constituted the act under which Philadelphia was governed until recent times.

During his service on the bench, from the beginning of 1882 until the summer of 1887, the most notable case tried before Judge Boyer was that of John M. Wilson, charged with murdering his employer, Anthony Dealy, of Wyndmoor.

One day in March, 1884, a boy gathering driftwood along the banks of the Wissahickon, near Thomas' Mill road, two miles below the county line, discovered a sack in the water, and the sack on being opened revealed the trunk of a man, the head, arms and legs having been cut off. In May following a human head was found imbedded in the mud nearby.

At the Philadelphia morgue the head was identified as that of Frederick Stahl, a Philadelphia butcher, who had disappeared in October, 1883. Stahl's brother and a friend made the identification. C. A. Dieterle, for whom Stahl had worked, was arrested, it being asserted that he had bags like those in which the dismembered body was found, that the body had been cut up with a butcher's cleaver and that Dieterle had been seen driving through Germantown toward the Wissahickon shortly after Stahl disappeared. At the trial Dieterle was acquitted.

One day more than two years after the body had been found in the Wissahickon a man giving his name as John M. Wilson surrendered to the police in Chicago, saying that in January, 1884, he had killed his employer, a farmer near Chestnut Hill, had cut up the body and thrown the fragments into the Wissahickon.

As there was no record of such a crime and as the Stahl identification had never been questioned, the police at first believed Wilson was seeking a free ride to Philadelphia. When full details of Wilson's confession arrived the name of the farmer he said he had killed was given as Anthony W. Dealy, of Springfield township, near Wyndmoor.

New inquiries now revealed that Dealey had disappeared in January, 1884, but it was supposed he had absconded because of financial troubles. His house was burned about the time of his disappearance. Wilson had been working for Dealy, but no suspicions as to a crime had ever been aroused.

Wilson was tried in March, 1886. The evidence was entirely circumstantial, such as his own confession suggested. After a trial continuing seven days he was convicted. On January 13, 1887, he paid the death penalty on the scaffold.

Wilson's confession narrated that Dealey could not pay his wages, which caused numerous quarrels. On the night of January 26, 1884, Wilson came into the house and found Dealy asleep on a lounge. Wilson then seized a cleaver and killed Dealy with a blow on the head. The next day, Sunday, he cut up the body, placed the parts in sacks and carried them at night to the Wissahickon in a sleigh, tossing them from the bridge at Bell's Mill road.

Wilson remained at the Dealy farm several days longer, sold some of the cattle, spent the money in dissipation and then set the house on fire and left, wandering about the country until remorse drove him to confess in Chicago.

Judge Boyer's death occurred suddenly August 16, 1887, at his home, on Sandy street. At 4 p. m., he was sitting in his library, apparently as well as usual. An hour later a servant found his dead body in the hallway. A stroke of apoplexy had caused death. He was buried at West Laurel Hill cemetery.

Judge Boyer came from Pennsylvania German stock, he having been born in New Hanover township in 1822. He was named for his maternal grandfather, Benjamin Markley, who had been one of the associate judges of the county. The father, General Philip Boyer, was an officer of the militia and was elected sheriff of the county in 1822. The son's boyhood was spent in Pottstown. He was educated at Lafayette College, Easton, and the University of Pennsylvania. He read law with Judge John M. Reed, in Carlisle, Pa., and began the practice of law in Norristown in 1844.

AARON S. SWARTZ

THIRTY-SIX years on the bench of Montgomery county, was the remarkable record attained by Judge Aaron S. Swartz—the longest period of service by any judge in the county. If Judge Swartz's career could be computed in terms of work accomplished, it would be indeed amazing, for his capacity for unremitting labor was prodigious.

Judge Swartz was the first additional law judge appointed after the county became a judicial district for itself. He had been the Republican nominee for president judge, in 1881, against Judge Henry P. Ross, then sitting. Judge Ross was re-elected. On the death of Judge Ross, in 1882, Governor Hoyt appointed Charles H. Stinson judge, but at the election that fall the Democratic nominee, B. Markley Boyer, was elected, over Judge Stinson.

It became apparent after a few years that the duties of the bench in Montgomery county were too much for one man. The Legislature of 1887 created the office of additional law judge for the county, and Governor James A. Beaver appointed Aaron S. Swartz to the position.

Judge Swartz came from a Mennonite family that had lived in the neighborhood of Towamencin township since colonial times. He was born on a farm in that township in 1849, was educated at Freeland Seminary, now Ursinus College, and at Lafayette College, Easton. For a short time he taught school in Phoenixville. Then he was appointed a deputy clerk in the United States District Court and at the same time he read law with Gilbert R. Fox, in Norristown, being admitted to the bar in 1875.

He soon became active in politics. In 1877 he was the Republican nominee for district attorney. Defeat was to be expected, but the fact that he lost by only 300 votes made the defeat almost a victory. For some years before his appointment as judge he was solicitor for the county commissioners.

Judge Swartz was commissioned additional law judge May 2, 1887. On August 20 following President Judge B. Markley Boyer died. Thereupon Judge Swartz succeeded to the president judgeship. In November, 1887, he was elected for the full ten-year term as president judge, and every decade following, up to 1917, he was re-elected, usually without opposition, the Democrats recognizing his pre-eminent fairness as a judge by refraining from making nominations for his office.

Of the great mass of litigation which required his adjudication during his long period of service it is almost impossible to speak in detail. But no matter how trivial or how important the case, Judge Swartz always gave the matters at issue the most thorough consideration. Questions of human values were never lost amidst mazes of legal verbiage. He viewed every angle of the issue. Considering the great number of cases which he heard, reversals of his decisions at the hands of higher courts were exceedingly few.

Unquestionably the case which attracted the greatest popular attention during Judge Swartz's term and which was probably the most sensational ever tried in the courts of Montgomery county was that growing out of the murder of Mrs. Charles O. Kaiser, in 1896.

One night in October of that year Frank Mancill was traveling along Crooked lane, in Upper Merion township, south of Bridgeport, when he met a highly excited man who declared highwaymen had attacked him and his wife as they were driving along the road in a buggy. The man, who proved to be Charles O. Kaiser, showed a bullet wound in his arm. In the carriage was found the dead body of Mrs. Kaiser, she having been shot through the head.

The Norristown police, with the aid of Detective Frank Geyer, of Philadelphia, soon concluded that the story of an attempted robbery was fiction. Kaiser, who had come to Norristown some time before that and opened a store here, was arrested. Benjamin Hughes reported he had seen a man walking toward the Kaiser carriage, while some distance away was another carriage in which a woman was seated. A revolver and Mrs. Kaiser's jewelry were found hidden under a stone near the scene of the tragedy.

Kaiser was tried before Judge Swartz in March, 1897, the trial consuming two weeks. The court room was thronged at every session, and newspapers all over the country printed reports of the case. So arduous were his duties that it was said Judge Swartz lost 14 pounds in weight during those two weeks.

District Attorney Jacob A. Strassburger was aided by Ex-District Attorney James B. Holland, afterwards United States District judge, and his law partner, John M. Dettra, and with the testimony of Detective Geyer they presented convincing evidence to show that Kaiser, James A. Clemmer and Elizabeth DeKalb had concocted a plot to kill Mrs. Kaiser after her life had been insured for $11,000. In the role of a highwayman Clemmer approached the Kaisers on the Upper Merion road and shot Mrs. Kaiser, Kaiser also being slightly wounded to give plausibility to the robbery story.

Kaiser was represented by N. H. Larzelere, Harry N. Brownback and M. M. Gibson, of Norristown, and G. Bradford Carr, of Philadelphia.

Kaiser was found guilty, and after a fruitless appeal to the Supreme Court he was sentenced to be hanged on September 6, 1898. He cheated the gallows on August 18, in his cell in the county prison, by cutting arteries in his arms and legs with a piece of a clock spring.

Elizabeth DeKalb and Clemmer were both arrested in November, 1897, the former in Philadelphia and the latter in Newark, N. J. The woman confessed the conspiracy. Clemmer was tried in June, 1898, District Attorney Jacob A. Strassburger conducting the prosecution, with the aid of James B. Holland, former district attorney, who had had charge of the Kaiser prosecution. By this time popular interest in the crime had greatly abated, and the excitement was not nearly so intense as at the time of Kaiser's trial. Kaiser and Elizabeth DeKalb both testified against Clemmer. He was convicted after a trial continuing eleven days. Clemmer was hanged in the county prison on May 18, 1899.

Elizabeth DeKalb pleaded guilty to being an accessory after the fact. She was sent to prison for two years.

Clemmer was represented by H. M. Brownback and Edward F. Kane. Miss DeKalb was represented by J. P. Hale Jenkins.

While Judge Swartz was on the bench the court house erected in the fifties of the nineteenth century was rebuilt and enlarged and a dome replaced the earlier steeple. This work, whereby the court house attained its present proportions, was in progress from May 1902, until June, 1904. During that time the sessions of the court were held in the building of the Historical Society of Montgomery County, on Penn street, adjoining the Public Square.

Beyond his duties on the bench Judge Swartz had two interests that strongly appealed to him. One was trout fishing. Almost every year he was out whipping some trout stream at the opening of the season. His other interest concerned the welfare of the First Presbyterian church. There he was a ruling elder and superintendent of the Sunday school for many years. He was often called upon to deliver addresses at religious assemblages.

Early in 1923, Judge Swartz's health failed so seriously that he was constrained to take advantage of a law passed a short time before that authorizing the retirement of judges. His death followed on August 28 of the same year.

HENRY K. WEAND

THE office of additional law judge for Montgomery county was created by the Legislature of 1887, and Governor Beaver appointed Aaron S. Swartz. In a few months President Judge B. Markley Boyer died, and Judge Swartz became president judge. Then Governor Beaver appointed Henry K. Weand to succeed Judge Swartz as additional law judge.

The voters at subsequent elections manifested their approval of the governor's appointment. Judge Weand was elected for the ten-year term in 1888, and was re-elected in 1898 and 1908.

Like Judge Swartz and Judge Boyer, Judge Weand was of Pennsylvania German lineage. He was born in Pottstown in 1838. Judge Boyer was his legal preceptor. He became a member of the bar in 1860.

Several judges of this district have been military men, but Judge Weand saw more active military campaigning than any of the others.

When President Lincoln's first call for troops came, in April, 1861, Henry K. Weand, then just establishing himself in a law practice, joined the Fourth Pennsylvania Volunteers, under command of Colonel John F. Hartranft. This was the first body of troops that left Norristown for service in the war. Mr. Weand was made first lieutenant in Company K.

The Fourth Regiment was mustered in for only three months' duty. In 1862 Mr. Weand enlisted as a private in the Fifteenth Pennsylvania Cavalry. This was a three-year regiment, and Mr. Weand remained with it until it was mustered out, in June, 1865. Meanwhile he had risen from private to captain of Company H.

The regiment made a splendid record. Soon after organization it was engaged in the battle of Antietam.

Then it was on duty in Tennessee, Alabama, Mississippi and elsewhere with the western armies. The commander was Colonel W. J. Palmer, afterwards widely known as the founder of Colorado Springs, Col.

As a resident of Norristown after the Civil War, Mr. Weand worked for the success of the Republican Party during the seventies when that party had but slight chance of victory in local campaigns. Twice he was the party's unsuccessful nominee for district attorney. Several times he was delegate to state conventions. He saw long service as a member of the Norristown School Board, and was president of the board. At different times he was solicitor for the county commissioners, for the Town Council of Norristown and for the sheriff.

His interest in military matters continued. In 1873 Governor John F. Hartranft made Mr. Weand judge advocate general on the governor's staff. Thus he was accorded the rank of brigadier general.

Many important cases were tried before Judge Weand during his service of 27 years as additional law judge. Often he and Judge Swartz sat together in the adjudication of weighty questions. They thus presided jointly in the trial of James A. Clemmer, in 1898, for the murder of Mrs. Charles O. Kaiser. Judge Weand, however, usually ruled on questions raised in that trial, and he delivered the charge to the jury.

The death of Judge Weand occurred on July 31, 1914, at Wernersville, Berks county, where he had gone for medical treatment, his health having failed some months prior to his death.

JOHN FABER MILLER

ALL the judges appointed or elected to the bench in Montgomery county in the nineteenth century had received their legal training in the office of one of the members of the bar. Toward the end of the century the old custom of reading law with a lawyer in established practice went out of vogue. Young men preparing to take up law as a profession studied in the law school of one of the large universities. Usually, though, they maintained nominal connection with the office of some practicing lawyer who was recognized as the preceptor of the student.

The first judge of the county whose training was that of the law school was Judge John Faber Miller. He was appointed additional law judge in 1914, upon the death of Judge Weand.

His name suggests Judge Miller's noteworthy Montgomery county lineage, for he was a descendant of the two John Fabers who were both beloved pastors of the Old and New Goshenhoppen Reformed charge, in the upper end of the county. John Theobold Faber held the pastorate from 1766 until 1779 and again from 1786 until his death in 1788. His son of the same name was educated for the ministry and upon ordination succeeded to the charge his father had served. Like him he was once tempted to take another pastorate but returned after some years to his first charge, and remained there until his death, in 1833. Both of the Fabers died suddenly while conducting funeral services.

The younger Faber married into the Arndt family, another distinguished pioneer family of Pennsylvania. His daughter married John Miller, a carpenter, of Pennsburg, who is said to have established the first English school in that place, himself employing a teacher and giving the use of his carpenter shop for the school. William G. Miller, a son of John Miller, who engaged in business in Philadelphia, was the father of Judge Miller.

Through his mother Judge Miller could trace his ancestry to another element that was prominent in the settlement of Montgomery county—the Welsh Quakers of the Gwynedd region. His mother was Caroline Roberts, daughter of Charles Roberts, a farmer and teacher in Whitpain township. The Roberts homestead, where six generations of the family have lived since 1764, is on Skippack pike, opposite the Whitpain Township High School, between Blue Bell and Center Square. Judge Miller bought the property shortly before he was elevated to the bench.

While he had rightful pride in his ancestry, Judge Miller recognized that it in itself gave him no special privileges in society. He discussed the subject in an address which he delivered in 1925 at the dedication of a tablet in the Old Goshenhoppen church commemorating the services of the early pastors of that church. On that occasion he said:

"It is not in the sense of hero worship that we should regard our ancestors. A man who points with pride to his ancestors and does nothing himself is not even to be respected. The accomplishments of our forebears should give us something to live up to and should be an inspiration and aspiration to go and do likewise."

Judge Miller was born in 1865 while his family lived at Weldon, in Abington township, but they soon afterward moved to the maternal homestead in Whitpain, where John Faber Miller spent his youth. He was graduated from the University of Pennsylvania and was admitted to the Philadelphia bar in 1886. In 1892 he began practicing in Norristown, being associated first with Charles Hunsicker and later with Samuel H. High. From 1909 until 1914 he was solicitor to the county commissioners.

Judge Miller held the office of additional law judge from his appointment by Governor Tener, in November, 1914, until the retirement of Judge Swartz, in 1923, when he became president judge.

Both in his law practice and in his judicial duties Judge Miller made use of modern labor-saving devices that tend toward methodical and thorough administration. All his own notes of cases which he heard were carefully filed in cabinets, so that in a moment he could get the essential facts about any of them.

It fell to the lot of Judge Miller to supervise an innovation in legal procedure when women, having gained the right to vote, were also required to serve as jurors. His tactfulness and discretion were of marked help in enabling the women to assume their new responsibilities in the courts.

Judge Miller's principal recreation was golf. For a time he was president of the Plymouth Country Club.

During his earlier years at the bar he lived in Springfield township, at Chestnut Hill, but on becoming judge he made his home in the former house of Joel Cook, on Sandy street, beyond the Norristown borough line.

His death occurred suddenly, like that of the two Fabers whose name he bore. After a day on the bench he went home on the evening of February 19, 1926, the day following his 61st birthday anniversary, and a few hours later was stricken with apoplexy, death being a quick result.

J. Ambler Williams

WHEN Judge Aaron S. Swartz retired from the bench, April 2, 1923, Judge John Faber Miller was advanced to president judge. To fill the vacancy Governor Pinchot appointed J. Ambler Williams, on April 17. He was elected for a ten-year term that year and upon the death of Judge Miller, in 1926, became president judge.

Judge Williams went upon the bench of the Montgomery county court in the prime of life, when little over half the normal span allotted to man.

For 19 years before election to the bench, Mr. Williams had practiced at the bar of the Montgomery county courts. From the start he commanded attention, especially because of his ability as a trial lawyer. Whenever he came before the bar it was evident he had prepared himself to meet anything that might arise in the trial of a cause; or, if in argument, he was ready with authorities to back his contention.

His ability as a lawyer is spread over the records of the courts. In the nearly score of years from the day he was graduated from the Law School of the University of Pennsylvania until he went upon the bench he had a large share of legal business and the experience thus gained, varied in all courts, has served as a substantial foundation for his judicial services. He gave up an extensive practice to assume the judicial role and is serving at a great financial sacrifice.

While busy along the lines of his profession, including much reading to keep up with ever-changing laws, he found time to care for physical needs on tennis court and golf course, so that he is physically as well as mentally fit for arduous labor.

Long recognized as an outstanding orator among the lawyers of the county and recognized, too, as pos-

sessed of wide knowledge of the law and an enviable
command of English, coupled withal by a voice well
modulated, easily understood and pleasing to the ear,
Judge Williams has demonstrated he is well qualified
for the judiciary.

Aside from other qualifications, Judge Williams is
possessed of a most equable disposition. He possesses
the "judicial temperament" element of mental calibre
or fibre to the highest degree.

Before coming to the bench, Judge Williams had
gained a reputation both as an orator and athlete.
Many of the judges of the county have been able
orators but none before was ever noted in sports.

As a law student at the University of Pennsylvania he was captain of the university's law school
football team in 1901. Previously he had been president of the Colgate University Athletic Association.
In 1908-9 he was coach of the football team of the
Norristown High School. He won tennis champion-
ships at the Ersine Tennis Club, Norristown, in 1910,
1911 and 1912, and at the Plymouth Country Club in
1912, 1913 and 1914. Later he transferred his devotion to golf.

While still a student in the Norristown High
School, in the late nineties, his gifts in public speaking
became evident. Graduating from the high school, in
1897, he entered Colgate University, where he won the
first senior debate prize and was selected by the faculty
as one of the six graduates to speak at the 1901 com-
mencement. Then as a law student at the University
of Pennsylvania he won first honors on debating teams.

Beginning the practice of law in 1904, politics
early engaged his interest. When yet a student at
Colgate he had taken the lead in organizing a McKinley
and Roosevelt Club among the students. In 1904 he
stumped the state in the presidential campaign and
was a frequent speaker in subsequent campaigns.
During the World War Mr. Williams was one of the
"four-minute" men; was a member of the legal ad-
visory board of the Norristown Draft Board, although

he resigned later to accept appointment as government appeal agent; and was legal adviser to the Pennsylvania State Council of National Defense for Montgomery county.

Those who recall the graceful eloquence of Judge Williams' father see the influence of heredity in Judge Williams' popularity as a speaker. Rev. Dr. Charles F. Williams, father of Judge Williams, was trained for the Baptist ministry and gained high favor as a preacher. Unfortunately, an affliction of the vocal organs placed him under the necessity of forsaking the ministry.

Judge Williams was born in Bridgeport in 1881, while his father was pastor of the Bridgeport Baptist church. After Dr. Williams' retirement from the pulpit the family lived in Norristown, Dr. Williams being president of James Lees and Sons Company, Bridgeport.

Though he has served only about half of his term, Judge Williams' course on the bench has won him high distinction, not alone in Montgomery county but throughout the legal profession of the state. This was evident when Chief Justice von Moschzisker, of the Pennsylvania Supreme Court, last year appointed Judge Williams member of a judicial committee to consider changes in laws to be submitted to the State Crime Commission with a view toward checking crime. More recently further recognition came to Judge Williams in connection with this same commission when he was made chairman of a sub-committee to draft certain proposed legislation.

One of the important problems with which Judge Williams has been concerned the last year and which will require his attention for some time to come is that of providing adequate space and facilities for the transaction of the county's business. With the tremendous growth of population the work of the courts and other departments of the county has grown by leaps and bounds, so that now the county has begun enlargement of the court house. To all details of plans Judge

Williams has given careful consideration, in order that preparations might be well thought out and matured ere actual construction should commence.

HAROLD G. KNIGHT

APPOINTMENT of an additional law judge for Montgomery county became necessary in 1926, when Judge John Faber Miller died and Judge J. Ambler Williams succeeded him as president judge. For the vacant additional law judgeship Governor Pinchot on March 4, 1926, named Harold G. Knight, of Ambler.

Those who knew of the extensive law practice which Judge Knight enjoyed up to 1926 realized that he accepted the honor conferred upon him at a considerable financial sacrifice. He had not been remarkably conspicuous in politics and had never been a candidate for office. But he was solicitor for the borough of Ambler, for the Ambler school district and for several townships and he had many desirable clients in Philadelphia and Montgomery county.

From the time of his admission to the bar, in 1902, until 1921, he had an office in Philadelphia. For a time he was associated in the law practice there with Raymond MacNeille, who was later president judge of the Municipal Court of Philadelphia and is now on the Common Pleas bench in that city. In conjunction with Howard J. Dager he also built up an extensive real estate business at Ambler with which he was identified for five years.

The appointment of Mr. Knight as additional law judge by Governor Pinchot met with general approval. This was further reflected in his election, without opposition, for a full ten-year term.

Mr. Knight is a self-made man who has risen to eminence by sheer ability and industry. His endorsement by his fellow lawyers was evidence of the impression he made at the Montgomery county bar and undoubtedly was a contributing factor in his elevation to the bench.

In Judge Knight President Judge Williams has an able and unquestionably an entirely satisfactory colleague and Judge Knight's career upon the bench has already merited ranking with the distinguished figures of the past in Montgomery county's judiciary.

Those who know Judge Knight intimately, and even many who know him only casually, realize he has exceptional ability as a jurist. He is widely informed in the literature of the law, is actuated at all times by the highest sense of duty and is possessed of a keen and accurate application of justice in all his work.

He is a man of decisive and outspoken opinion but considerate and courteous at all times on and off the bench.

He, like Judge Williams, has remarkable physical powers which aid inestimably in fulfillment of the mental demands made in judicial work.

His popularity brought about his election to the presidency of numerous organizations, among them the Ambler Athletic Association, the Sunnyside Alumni Association, the Wissahickon Fire Company of Ambler, the Ambler Branch of the Red Cross, the North Penn Community Center and the Ambler Rotary Club, while he was also a director in several financial enterprises. As a speech-maker few Montgomery county men have been in greater demand than Judge Knight.

Judge Knight is a member of a family that has been prominently identified with the growth of the Ambler region since the middle of the nineteenth century. George Knight, a native of Philadelphia and the grandfather of Judge Knight, bought 45 acres along Butler pike in 1854. This territory now comprises the business district of Ambler. But in 1854 there was no Ambler. A little settlement that was the nucleus of the future town was called Wissahickon.

Later George Knight also owned the principal store in Ambler and the lumber and coal yard adjoining.

George Knight's daughter, Elizabeth, founded Sunnyside Boarding and Day School, in Ambler, which attained a high reputation as an educational institution in the days before public schools had become well developed. Her sisters, Sara A. and Cordelia E., assisted as teachers in the school. In this school under the tutelage of his aunts Judge Knight received his early education.

He was born in 1880, the son of Alexander Knight, one of six children of George Knight. Alexander Knight still lives in Ambler, where he has long been a director of the First National Bank of Ambler.

The Knight family has lived in Pennsylvania since the province was founded by William Penn, for the first of the family was Giles Knight, who, with his wife and their two-year-old son, came to America with Penn on the ship Welcome.

WILLIAM F. SOLLY

UP to 1901 judges of the Montgomery county courts were required to conduct any and every kind of court that could be held in the county—Common Pleas, Quarter Sessions, Criminal Court and Orphans' Court. In that year the Legislature authorized the establishment of a separate Orphans' Court in Montgomery county. In compliance with a petition bearing the signatures of 67 of the 72 members of the Montgomery county bar, Governor Stone appointed William F. Solly president judge of the new court.

Judge Solly during all his public career was noted for his talents as an organizer. Hence, the organizing of the new court, a duty of the highest importance, was most capably performed.

Judge Solly continued to serve on the bench of the Orphans' Court until his death, in 1927, he being re-elected to office in 1911 and 1921 without opposition.

His court lacked the public interest attached to many of the suits tried in the other courts. Great burdens of routine detail are attached to the settlement of estates. All of this received faithful attention at the hands of Judge Solly. Occasionally he also assisted the other judges in conducting criminal court.

However, the Orphans' Court is not without its share of problems possessed of wide human appeal. One such question upon which Judge Solly ruled in 1924 concerned the right of a decedent to attach religious qualifications to a bequest. A woman living near Bethayres bequeathed $15,000 in trust for the use of a niece but stipulated that the trust should cease if the niece ever forsook the Protestant faith. The niece became a Catholic. But Judge Solly held that she was entitled to the bequest, declaring "the conditions attached to the trust violate public policy and are contrary to law." He reviewed the history of the movement to accord every citizen the right to worship according to the dictates of his conscience, and it was his opinion that the conditions of the will were an attempt to punish the niece if her religion was not such as met her aunt's approval.

In another will contest, in 1909, Judge Solly ruled on the validity of the custom of disinheriting heirs mentioned in a will if they contested the will. A woman living in Hatboro left an estate believed to have been worth $100,000. To a score or more of her relatives she made bequests of $500 or $1000 each, and the residue was to go to her business agent. Some of the relatives contested the will on the ground that the testatrix was mentally incapable and was subjected to undue influence. They lost in the Orphans' Court and also upon appeal to the Supreme Court. Then the executor went before Judge Solly to determine whether the $500 and $1000 legacies should be paid, as a clause of the will provided that any heirs who contested the will should receive nothing. Judge Solly decided that all the bequests should be paid, declaring "there was a reasonable and probable cause for the contest."

Judge Solly came to the bench after a ripe experience as a lawyer and an active participant in public affairs. He was the first man appointed to the bench all of whose life had been spent in Norristown. Here he was born in 1858, the son of Benjamin F. Solly, a shoe merchant. He was graduated from the Norristown High School in 1873, and he "read law," according to the old-time methods, in the office of the elder Gilbert R. Fox, being admitted to the bar in 1879.

He was solicitor for various townships and for several county offices. He was counsel for the State Hospital trustees and for the Valley Forge Park Commission. After the death of former Judge Charles H. Stinson, in 1899, Mr. Solly became counsel for the Pennsylvania Railroad in Montgomery county.

When electric light was introduced, in the late eighties, he was one of the incorporators of the Norristown Electric Light and Power Company. He was also an incorporator of the Albertson Trust Company and its president for a time. The diversity of his interests may be understood from the fact that he was president of the old Norristown Library Company, the Montgomery County Fish, Game and Forestry Association and the Norristown Club.

For many years prior to his elevation to the bench he was foremost among the workers for the success of the Republican party. From 1880 until 1892 he was secretary of the Republican County Committee, and for the ensuing nine years he was county chairman, effecting thorough organization of the party in every district of the county and firmly establishing the political supremacy of the party.

J. BURNETT HOLLAND

JUDGE W. F. Solly died June 20, 1927. Thereupon Governor Fisher appointed J. Burnett Holland to the vacant place on the Orphans' Court bench.

The appointment was made June 27, 1927, and Mr. Holland took the oath of Judgeship on July 1, 1927. He served by appointment until the first Monday of January, 1928, when he began his 10-year term, having been elected on the Republican and Democratic tickets in November, 1927.

During the short time Judge Holland has fulfilled the the duties of his office, his work has carried conviction among all concerned that he will honorably maintain the splendid record set by his predecessor.

Judge Holland, who was born in Conshohocken in 1887, is the son of the late Judge James B. Holland, who was a judge of the Federal Courts from 1904 until his death, in 1914, and who prior to his ascension to the bench was Republican county chairman. The son was graduated from the Law School of the University of Pennsylvania and entered the bar in 1912.

Judge Holland served almost two years in the World War as a private in the 312th Machine Gun Battalion, attached to the 79th Division.

Resuming the practice of law, he was appointed second assistant district attorney of Montgomery county in 1920, and in 1924 he was promoted to first assistant district attorney. He held that office at the time of his elevation to the bench, July 1, 1927.

Governor Fisher, as recommended by Secretary of Commonwealth Charles Johnson, placed the toga of the late Judge Solly, president judge of the Orphans' Court of Montgomery County, upon Mr. Holland, of Norristown.

It was a popular appointment. This was evident by the flood of congratulations poured from all parts of the county. The messages were also tinged with expressions of confidence in his ability and praiseworthy comment upon his qualifications.

However, it was not mere popularity that actuated Secretary Johnson to recommend Mr. Holland for the judgeship. Mr. Johnson knows an Orphans' Court judge must not only have a firm grip on a wide range of legal affairs but must have a great breadth of understanding of the law and be capable of using it most intelligently.

Personally acquainted with Mr. Holland ever since he was admitted to the Montgomery County Bar 15 years ago, Mr. Johnson always admired the spirit, the courage, the principles of Mr. Holland. Initial recognition of these qualities came in January, 1920, when Mr. Holland was named second assistant district attorney under District Attorney Frank X. Renninger. Four years later promotion to first assistant district attorney under Mr. Renninger was proof of the efficiency that had marked his service in the public prosecutor's office.

In July, 1927, a higher estimate was placed upon Mr. Holland's ability by Secretary Johnson, and this estimate was promptly endorsed by the chief executive of Pennsylvania by appointment to the vacancy on the Orphans' Court Bench of this county.

In one respect Judge Holland is perhaps unique among jurists. He is a singer of wide reputation, and is frequently heard as a soloist. He first attracted attention as a choir singer. Then he achieved many a success in opera roles and also in amateur theatricals. He is now a member of the Philadelphia Civic Opera Company, and takes part in the performances of that organization.

GEORGE C. CORSON

ON March 6, 1929, Governor Fisher appointed Assistant District Attorney George C. Corson as additional law judge of the 38th Judicial District of Pennsylvania, comprised of Montgomery County, immediately after signing the bill sponsored by Mrs. Mabelle Kirkbride, first assemblywoman of Montgomery County, creating a new judgeship in this county.

The appointment of Mr. Corson to the bench by Governor Fisher was made upon recommendation of Secretary of Commonwealth Charles Johnson.

Friday, March 8, Attorney Corson was elevated to the Bench, the oath of office being administered by President Judge Williams before an assemblage of judges, lawyers, state, county and local officials and a host of admiring relatives and friends.

The services of Mr. Corson as assistant district attorney had been notable and merited the popular appointment.

Mr. Corson had proved that in legal circles there is much he can do—and do it thoroughly, capably, fearlessly and honestly. His skill, his tact, his knowledge of law, his high sense of justice all qualified him for the important office and presaged a successful career as a member of our judiciary.

Mr. Corson won admiration and commendation from jurors, lawyers and judges by his work in the county courts, and his experience as a trial lawyer and in arguing cases gave him an unusually thorough training for service on the Bench.

George C. Corson resides at Plymouth Meeting, and has resided there all his life. He was born on September 9, 1889, and was 39 years of age last birthday.

He was educated at Friends Central School, Philadelphia; Swarthmore College, and was graduated from Law School University of Pennsylvania in 1914.

Mr. Corson was admitted to practice before the Supreme Court of Pennsylvania and the Courts of Montgomery County in 1914 and practiced law in Norristown until May, 1917, when he enlisted in the Reserve Corps of the U. S. Regular Army, and was called into active service in the Motor Transport Corps at Camp Meade, Maryland, in July, 1917. Later he was transferred to Camp Johnson, Jacksonville, Florida, and when commissioned second lieutenant was assigned to the 90th Division at San Antonio, Texas.

Attorney Corson went to France with this division and served six months overseas. He was made a first lieutenant just prior to the Armistice, and served with the same division in the Army of Occupation in Germany until May 21, 1919, when the division returned to the United States, and he was discharged at Camp Dix on June 16, 1919.

Mr. Corson returned to the practice of law at Norristown, and became an assistant district attorney under District Attorney Frank X. Renninger in January, 1920. In 1924, when Mr. Renninger was re-elected, Mr. Corson became second assistant district attorney, and in the Spring of 1928, he was appointed first assistant district attorney when J. Burnett Holland was made President Judge of the Orphans' Court.

Mr. Corson was one of the secretaries of the Montgomery County Republican Committee for some years, and upon the death of J. Crawford Johnson became chairman of the County Committee.

He is a member of the Fritz Lodge of Masons; Plymouth Meeting Society of Friends; Norristown Club; Order of Founders and Patriots; Pennsylvania State Grange; Delta Theta Phi Law Fraternity and Phi Delta Theta College Fraternity.

He is a son of George and Elizabeth Cadwallader Corson of Plymouth Meeting, and is a great great nephew of Dr. Hiram Corson. His family has resided in Montgomery County for more than a century.

Index

CPSIA information can be obtained
at www.ICGtesting.com
Printed in the USA
BVHW072317051218
534639BV00052B/704/P